Create the NEW YOU

TAKE BACK CONTROL OF YOUR LIFE

YOUR POCKET GUIDE TO FREEDOM

"IT'S NOT THE STRONGEST OF THE SPECIES THAT SURVIVES,

NOR THE MOST INTELLIGENT THAT SURVIVES.

IT'S THE ONE THAT IS THE MOST ADAPTABLE TO CHANGE"

~Charles Darwin

CONTENTS

INTRODUCTION

I have had the pleasure of meeting and working with some of the most brilliant minds and individuals. They range from CEOs of multinationals, university Professors, doctors, professional sports stars, senior and middle managers, ordinary people, single mothers, drug users and every type of person in between.

All of whom had the same problem, **FEAR** of change, in various degrees. They wanted to change because their situation was unsustainable or unbearable. But they couldn't, because they didn't know how to, or were unsure of the next step to take, due to being immersed in, or emotionally tied to their current situation.

As a private mentor and business consultant, my role is to find a solution to their issues and provide them with a plan, strategy, roadmap or blueprint. We worked together on delivering a mechanism that was right for them, to remove and overcome their emotional challenges, limiting beliefs, financial burdens and other obstacles that were holding them back. .

I did not tread lightly around egos or tip toe around their insecurities, to make people feel better and provide a generic, one size fits all solutions. No, I challenged their thought processor, belief systems, interrupted those destructive patterns and asked questions they never thought of, to assist them to become a new and an improved version of themselves.

Our thoughts determine what we believe, what we believe determines our feelings, how we feel influences our actions. This cycle then produces the results, if you want different results, you must change the cycle.

The purpose of this book is to highlight that whatever situation you currently find yourself in, all is not lost. It's time to CREATE THE NEW YOU and become the person you have always wanted to be.

Chapter One
GO BEYOND THE STATUS QUO

Does the world around you seem as though it makes no sense anymore? Or, maybe it never did. Do you struggle with feeling like, what's the point in trying, sad, or even worthless? Have you tried your hand at business or contributing your talents where you thought you belonged only to find out that maybe you were wrong?

Maybe none of these sad notions apply to you. Maybe you feel as though you have been somewhat of a success, but you strive for even more, greater things with even higher ambitions and want to know how to get there.

Regardless of whether you have come to this book at the lowest bottomless pit of your lifetime, or if you come to it in hopes of being propelled to even more success, if you could spend 7 days focused on changing one thing that would, in turn, change everything for the better, would you do it?

The fact remains that by the time you have read to the end, you will have a new and unlimited potential that will start with devoting just one week of your time. It all starts with a 7-day plan that is laid out in this pocket guide to freedom.

Use this practical pocket guide to change your life.

Whatever your dilemma, whether you are facing a life-changing, business-related decision or you're simply tired of feeling like the underdog, it's time to make a change. What if all it takes to change your circumstances is to change your diet? Only, we are not talking about what you put in your mouth to eat. Instead, this diet is going to involve feeding your brain differently. Since thoughts are what feed our thinking, it will mean changing the thoughts we choose to feed into our thinking, and it will only require you to focus on the thoughts you are feeding your mind for a full week. That's seven days to start the process of changing the world around you simply by feasting on healthier thoughts.

Think about putting thoughts into your head like you think about your diet, what you eat to fuel your body with calories and energy. It is common to eat three meals a day, breakfast, lunch, and dinner. Or, some call one of them supper depending upon which meal is the largest meal of the day. When you look at a newborn baby, however, they want to be fed about every two to four hours. Likewise, many diets intended to boost your metabolism are going to call for eating less food, more frequently which focuses on nutrition-packed power meals throughout the day.

Counting thoughts like we count calories

Just like counting calories on a diet to make sure we get the most nutrients for what we are allowing to go into our bodies, we must consider each and every thought. According to the Laboratory of Neuro-Imaging, it is estimated that we have about 70,000 thoughts a day. If we are thinking all day and night, that's about 2,916 thoughts an hour. In reality, we are probably thinking more thoughts than that each hour since we are not consciously thinking while we sleep. Regardless, that's a lot of thoughts that come into our heads on an hourly and daily basis.

During this 7-day exercise of thought shifting and re-shaping, really pay close attention to the quality of the thoughts you are allowing into your mind. Allowing time to sleep when we are not consciously putting effort into what we are feeding our thinking, that leaves about 4,375 thoughts per waking hour that the average person thinks. Even if you start by simply focusing only on about one percent of these thoughts, that's still quite a bit of thinking.

Let's start the 7-day thought replacement plan as you would begin a healthy diet. Only, with actual food, the intention will be to either shift nutrition value in the foods we are eating to focus on gaining more of the vitamins and minerals we need that are found in certain foods and not others. Whereas, this thought-changing program of 7 days will instead replace thinking that is holding us back and not currently doing us any good with thoughts that will propel us into a successful future.

Are you willing to give it a try?

First, you must realise a very important truth about who you are. You have the ability to develop new and unlimited potential. But, it's going to take a week of focused, challenging effort to achieve it.

If we do not like the things that are happening to us, this is a definite sign that it's time to change things. This starts by changing the way we think. These thoughts will be the very foundation on which we build the world around us.

You don't need to change the conditions around you. When you apply these laws, the conditions spontaneously change. You will have started the process of creating a paradigm shift from darkness of anxiety, depression, despair and low self esteem to one of hope, confidence optimism and a more fulfilling life. This new realisation of more confidence and self belief about who you truly are will lead you to a new found potential that you never thought possible. Are you ready to start?

Stop the vicious cause and effect cycle that leaves you feeling hopeless. Take back control of your life. Be the cause instead of allowing negative circumstances to effect the way you look at life. It all starts with one week of focused effort. If you want to transform your life and every component of it, including work, family, and friends, you must begin to train yourself to take control of your thoughts until it becomes a habit.

Here is how it's done

Let's start with an in-depth background or foundation with an explanation of terms just to make sure we are all on the same, level starting point. One concept to keep in mind is this:

The solution to any problem is usually a process that causes it to happen. Keeping emotions out of the process is an important skill to be learned in the process.

You must define the goal and hold the goal steady in your mind. Then, take control of the thoughts by accepting the help of events, inspiration, and focus. The process requires a lot of practice to become skillful.

What do we mean by change?

What do we mean by changing your circumstances? The word change is the process by which things become different. Other words to describe change include:

- **transition** - the process of changing from one situation, form, or state to another
- **transformation** - a change into someone or something completely different, or the process by which this happens
- **conversion** - the process of changing from one system, method, or use to another

- **adaptation** - the process of changing something so that it can be used for a different purpose
- **modification** - the process of changing something slightly, especially in order to improve it
- **alteration** - the process of making a change in the appearance or form of something
- **revision** - the process of changing, improving, or making additions to something such as a plan, law, or piece of writing
- **flux** - a condition of continuous change
- **refinement** - a small change that is made to something in order to improve it
- **game-changing** - completely changing the way that something is done, thought about, or made

Thoughts can be a curse or the cure.

The idea that thoughts can be a curse or the cure may sound a bit harsh, especially when you focus on that curse word. After all, why would anyone purposely put a curse on themselves? But, the truth is that when we decide to dwell on negativity instead of potential or the upside, we unknowingly turn our thoughts into a curse. On the other hand, when we opt for a more uplifting mindset or attitude, we bring about the cure to all of our problems and roadblocks in life and in business. Let's look at those two words in a little more detail.

A curse is not a good thing. Though, it doesn't require voodoo or witches stirring a cauldron speaking incantations. It is a result of harm or punishment. It could be an offensive word or a phrase that expresses annoyance or anger. It is a hindrance or a detriment. It is misfortune or something that brings about severe affliction or torment. Every culture or society places different criteria on what defines a curse word or foul language.

When these words are spoken they are called curse words or cursing. Cursing or curse words are often those spoken in haste and anger without considering their consequences.

A cure, on the other hand, is a remedy or a solution to a problem or illness. It is often used in a medical sense to explain how an illness was remedied and health has returned. It implies that relief has come or that health has been restored. A cure is a procedure that puts an end to suffering and allows healing or improvement to take place. To cure something is to make better or to make well, to cleanse.

It is also used to describe the process of preserving things, such as meat, by adding salt, drying, and then smoking it. To cure something means to let it sit in a salty solution. This definition is usually used in terms of making meat tasty. But, it can be applied to the resources in this book that will require 7 days to cure.

Our thoughts are more powerful than we realise. They can truly become a curse or be the cure to our circumstances.

Before you roll your eyes and walk away thinking this is some mind over matter solution that only works on the weak minded, tricking them into believing their world has changed. This is more than a smoke in mirror magic act, and it is no trick. Changing our thoughts really will change the world around us. It doesn't just change our perception of the world around us, though that is a good starting point. Purposefully transforming our thoughts in our minds literally begins to turn situations around.

When we dwell on negative, harmful or hurtful thoughts, they will begin to manifest in our physical lives as a curse would with its connotations hovering. These damaging words are always present almost as if they are waiting to pounce on any circumstance to prove they are right.

On the other hand, when we dwell on the more positive aspects of life, more pleasing things will begin to manifest in our physical lives as if medicine has been infused into our lives to heal all that is wrong. It is our choice to determine whether or not we will allow our thoughts to become a curse to our lives or to start the process of manifesting a cure in everything we encounter.

Relationships begin to either break apart or come together in light of what aspects we decide to focus on. Many claim that there is even a shift in their finances, either for the worse or for the better depending on where their focus rests to flourish or to fester.

Exercise your brain

Thinking, according to the Oxford English Dictionary and the American Heritage Dictionary, is forming in the mind. It includes symbol manipulation and deduction. Changing the thoughts we feast upon for a week won't just passively happen. It is going to take a lot of concerted effort. Train yourself to control each and every thought that comes into your head. This is extremely challenging at first, but like working a muscle in your physical body, the process becomes easier as you develop good habits.

When we exercise the muscles in our bodies, we do so in a different way depending on what our end goal is that we want to achieve. For instance, if we are just in it for some muscle tone and weight loss, our experience is going to be quite different than those who are in it to train for running a marathon. Either way, there are some basic steps for whatever kind of exercise we are putting our body through. These include starting early, starting small, and being aware of our limitations.

When we begin a workout routine, we might start out with light weights that offer just enough of a challenge but not too strenuous of an effort, or we will tire out too quickly and give up. We first assess our physical condition to make sure we are not overdoing it and are keeping pace with our goals. Trainers for a marathon typically begin about a year ahead of time to reach their goal.

For marathon trainers, they follow some basic steps of building up from their base mileage by devoting three to five times a week to running. These weekly runs will include completing a long run every 7 days or so giving your body time to gradually adjust to long distances. It will also include some speed work with practice intervals and tempo runs to increase cardio. And then, there is the rest and recovery that is just as important of a step to the process as the workout.

Another part of building healthy muscles in our bodies is to make sure we are eating the right foods. If you are in it to lose weight, you are going to start counting calories and feasting on low-calorie, low-fat foods that provide the most nutrients and make you feel full. This may actually mean eating more often throughout the day in a couple hour increments with nutrient-rich nibbles to boost our metabolism and give our muscles what they need to be healthy and shed the excess pounds.

Runners looking to complete a marathon have a different goal in mind. To attain this goal, they may feast on carbohydrates. Even during the marathon, there are stations they run passed where people are handing out foods rich in carbohydrates. They often do an extreme carb load before a run that might include a meal like spaghetti and other foods loaded with and rich in carbohydrates.

Training our thinking, or exercising our brains, is going to involve similar steps. And, since our thoughts are the food that keeps our minds working, the thoughts we choose to feed our minds are going to be a very important part of the exercise.

Before you take the first step into Day 1 of this 7-day plan to change, let's look at the reasoning behind the method and what makes it work. To fully understand what you will be doing and the concept behind how it works, it's important to look at it from as many angles as possible. For instance, for some, an analogy of computer programming may be needed to fully understand the 7-day steps to changing thinking patterns. For others, relating our thought life with the fuel that propels a jet engine or allows our automobiles to run smoothly may be what sparks the understanding. Let's take a look at both.

Reprogram your thinking

Maybe you're not an athlete and the idea of going to a gym or setting up a plan for a workout does not appeal to you in the least. Maybe, instead, you relate more to a logical, straightforward mindset. Take for instance, how a computer works.

Computers that we use everyday run on a program with well-written code. Whether it be a desktop, lap top, a smart phone we hold in our hands, or a programmed watch we wear on our wrist, someone programmed the device to respond the way it does. If something goes wrong with these devices, our first reaction is usually not to merely toss out the entire device. Instead, we reboot it. If that doesn't work, we go to the source and have it reprogrammed. This is the same thing we must do with our thoughts. It's like a programmer running a debugging program, step by step until we get the desired results.

It doesn't matter how much you paid for a fancy phone or laptop, if nothing has been programmed to make it work, it is worthless. On the other hand, if it has been skillfully programmed to run apps or to respond to your commands, it suddenly becomes very valuable. All of this is determined by what data we have fed it. In return, the device responds.

To get a bit technical, computing, in and of itself, is a process that is executed by a thread that contains the program code. Depending on which operating system you choose, this process could consist of several threads of execution. The program itself merely collects instructions. It is the process that executes, or puts the instructions into action.

For a computer program to run, there must first be machine code that is executable, memory, an operating system, security attributes, and a processor state or context. It all starts with the proper code, but part of the process includes security attributes which is a set of permissions, or allowable operations. First, the process is designed by being loaded from a secondary storage device into the main memory. After this, the process scheduler assigns it the waiting state. While the process is waiting, it is waiting for the scheduler to do a context switch. This context switch loads the process into the processor and changes the state to running. Processes frequently need to communicate to keep the process moving.

Before you feel baffled by all of this, the point is that this is very similar to how our brains work. We feed data, thoughts, into our mind at which point it needs to operate using a set of permissions to determine which thoughts will be allowed in. This requires the right kind of communication. The way our minds function from here can be switched from the negative thoughts we have allowed in up to this point into more productive thinking.

Programs are made up of sequences of instructions for processors. A single processor can only run one instruction at a time. When it is necessary, the program is stopped, and the operating system switches the processor to run another program.

A programming language for a computer is a vocabulary and set of rules that instruct the computer or computing device to perform specific tasks. Commands using BASIC or C# are going to be different than those using Java, FORTRAN, or a Pascal program. Each language has its own unique set of keywords that it understands and a special syntax for organising the programming instructions.

All levels of computing start with code, or a set of commands written in a language understood by the framework on which most developers use to write commands to perform specific applications. For those of you who understand programming, it doesn't take long before you determine which programming language is best to use for the program you want to run. If you are a gamer, you must first decide what platform you will build your game upon, and this will most likely determine which programming language you choose to write the most efficient code that will produce the fastest, most responsive, outcome.

Similarly, feeding our mind thoughts that are carefully developed to transform our thinking will reprogram the way we interact with the world around us. Like a computer running on data that a programmer has fed into it, we begin to function using the data we feed into our thoughts.

Debugging our thoughts

Likewise, in computer programming, if a problem is encountered, there is a debugging process that takes place. Debugging is done to detect and remove existing or potential errors, which are called bugs. These software bugs cause code to behave unexpectedly or to crash. Sometimes it takes more time to debug a program than it does to write the entire code in the first place.

To debug the program, the user begins with a problem, isolates the source code of the problem, and then fixes it. Once fixed, the software runs smoothly. Sometimes, resetting the program variables is what is needed to debug the code. If you have identified areas in your personal or business life that seems to not measure up to what you had hoped, it may be time to debug your thoughts and reset your variables with better thinking.

Fuel for thoughts

If your mind is boggled with the details and specifics related to computer programming languages, let's look instead at cars and aircraft. Fuel is like food for vehicles. It is what keeps them running. Like a car or an aircraft cannot run without the proper fuel, our minds run on the thoughts we pour into them. Let's take a look at how cars and airplanes, from race cars to jet planes, use fuel to run properly.

The purpose of the vehicle fuel system is to store and supply fuel to the engine. All fuel systems must supply fuel to the combustion chamber and control the amount of fuel that is supplied in relation to the amount of air. The engine then provides an intake system where the fuel is mixed with air, atomised, vaporised and compressed in the engine cylinder and ignited to produce energy or power.

Much like the way our lives are going will alert us to the fact that we need to readjust what thoughts we feed our minds, our vehicles will alert us to the awareness that fuel is not being distributed properly. For instance, the engine will have difficulty starting, become slow or hesitate upon acceleration, stall while driving, intermittently lose power, idle rough, or return decreased fuel efficiency.

In a jet aeroplane, a process of thrust that combines a process of air and fuel is what propels the plane forward. The engine moves the airplane forward with a great amount of force that is produced by a tremendous thrust. A jet engine is also sometimes referred to as a gas turbine. The engine sucks in air at the front fan. A compressor raises the pressure of the air. The blades on the compressor spin at a high speed to squeeze the air until it is compressed and sprayed with fuel. In the back of the engine, as the jets of gas shoot backward, the engine and the airplane are thrust forward.

Thrust is the force that pushes the aeroplane forward. As discovered by Sir Isaac Newton, for every action there is an equal and opposite reaction. It is upon this principle that airplanes move through the air. But, thrust cannot operate efficiently without the proper fuel.

Regardless of whether you are skilled at computer programming or have a love for flying or racing, these next 7 days are going to be the stepping off point in which you take the action needed for change. It all starts by changing our thoughts. The difference from this plan and other things you may have tried to improve your circumstances is that this 7-day process will literally begin to change things in your life. These changes will be real and not conjured up or perceived like a dream.

Change perspective – Change the outcome

There are many instances where someone finds themselves in a bad situation but learns to see the brighter side of life through adversity. One ancient tale comes to mind is that of the blind men and the elephant. The story goes like this paraphrased version:

There was a group of blind men who were told that an animal called an elephant was in town. None of them had ever encountered what an elephant was, so they went to inspect it through touch since they could not see. The first man, who had explored the trunk of the animal described an elephant as a thick snake. Another, who had explored the elephant's ear, said the animal was more like a fan. Still another blind man who had explored the animal's leg described an elephant as a pillar like a tree trunk.. Another, who had explored its tail, said that an elephant was like a rope. Another of the blind men described an elephant as a wall, after exploring the side of the animal. Finally, the one who had felt the tusk said that an elephant is hard and smooth like a spear.

Depending on who is telling the story, the point is going to be somewhat different. Regardless, the fact remains that all of them described this large animal based upon their perspective and personal experience of what they had felt. Their definition of an elephant was limited. Yet, the fact remained that the complete picture of these parts that made up the elephant was standing before them. They just could not see the big picture but only their individual perspectives.

Others may tell you stories that are rooted in historic truth and inspiration about how they faced hardships and came out on top. Though, these seven days you are about to embark upon will not only give you a better perspective of the hard times you are going through but will actually change your circumstances.

This 7-day project of changing your thoughts goes beyond that. While your eyes may be opened to grand things you never noticed before, you will not merely see things from a new perspective. At the end of your week long thought enriching process, your circumstances will actually begin to change for the better as you begin to change your thoughts.

Chapter Two
TAKE CONTROL OF YOUR DESTINY

Cause v Effect

Our senses are how we perceive the world around us. Yes, we can change our perception. Most wouldn't argue with that. But, there is more to it. When we begin to change the way we think, we begin to control the cause factor as well. It sounds a bit mysterious, but it's true. By changing our thoughts, we can change the world around us. To understand this better, we must first understand what is meant by cause and effect.

Cause and effect means that for everything that happens is the result of something. For instance, a cause and effect relationship is something that enables an event to occur. It is a concept used often in literature, stories, or in teaching children to write and to instill critical thinking.

For instance, if you leave an ice cube on a hot pavement, what will happen? If you forget to put on sunscreen and spend hours in the direct sunlight, what will happen? If you mix the colours yellow and blue, what colour do you make? If you fill an aeroplane with too much weight, what will happen? These are all examples of cause and effect scenarios.

Our thoughts are causative

If you did not have the capacity to change your state of mind and your thoughts, you would have no control over your thoughts whatsoever. Everything about your life would then be a result, or an effect, of something out of your control. But, it's not that way. You have the ability to turn your state of mind into a causative force. You must be determined to begin carefully choosing your every thought. Otherwise, turning your life into a success will be a hopeless effort.

Over the course of the next 7 days, you will begin to notice a cause and effect pattern in the world around you, and it's going to start by changing your thoughts.

We are not limited to mere physical cause and effect as if we are a victim of our circumstances. To the contrary, by changing the way we think, we actually influence actual physical change all around us. For instance, balanced thoughts don't just help us feel happy. They change the world around us to become more balanced. Instead of reacting and living constantly as part of the effect, put yourself in the cause. Bend reality into a different direction. This time, begin to shape a case-based reality. Instill balance and happiness in your thoughts so that it can then be expressed outwardly. In order for our thoughts to be the cause to a desired effect, we must change the way we think.

The way we think causes change to happen. Our thoughts are more than feelings that float in and out of our consciousness. They are actually a real, live causative force. Think about it. You cannot change your environment without first changing the way you think. If you change these thoughts, the world around you will have to follow suit and change as well. The way we think causes things to change in our environment. If we change our thinking, our conditions have to change as well.

Reality

There is a type of therapy and theory that is used by psychologists to help their patients gain control of their lives and attain goals by reshaping their behavior. It's called Reality Therapy and was developed by Dr. William Glasser in 1965. At its core, it is a form of therapy that aims to help people with unmet needs to set goals, problem solve, and create a more meaningful connection with others. It recognised five basic human needs that must be met for satisfaction in life. These five needs include survival, love and belonging, power, freedom, and fun or satisfaction, pleasure, enjoyment. The entire concept is based on something called Choice Theory that states all human behaviour is driven by the pursuit of fulfilling the five basic needs and all behaviour is a result of choices. In other words, our lives are the product of the choices we make. The same can be applied to the thoughts we decide to think. Similarly, Dr. Glasser encouraged clients to focus on the present and not on the past, avoid discussing symptoms, focus on changing thoughts and behavior, avoid criticising, blaming, or comparing oneself to others, avoid relying on excuses for behavior, and make specific plans with smart goals. (Specific - Measurable - Achievable - Relevant - Time-bound goals).

Over the next 7 days, you will begin to train your thinking to not only perceive things from a more positive outlook but to observe with all of your senses a real, objective change.

Objective thinking

There are two basic ways to approach any thought. One is subjective thinking, and the other is objective thinking. The difference between the two is basically that one makes decisions based on logic and proof, and the other interjects a personal viewpoint and feelings to direct the thinking process. We are so familiar with our thoughts, and they are so much a part of us that it is very difficult to look at them in an objective manner. Yet, actively choosing to change the way you think and shifting your state of mind is exactly what you must learn to do.

Objective thinking means that we base our thinking and reasoning upon a set of logically defined standards.

Subjective thinking refers to thinking and reasoning largely contingent on the individual.

Think of it this way, subjective thinking is subject to change. This may sound like thinking objectively is more like a robot without feeling, but that isn't really the case. Objective thinking is done with an open mind while it considers all of the facts as opposed to measuring every thought against a personal feeling.

A statement or line of thought is objective when it is based on facts, can be proven easily, or is impossible to deny. Although, without facts these thoughts or statements become subjective. A subjective thought is often interjected into a presentation when a speaker, for instance, presents his or her opinion. An opinion is always based on subjective thinking since it is from one perspective and based on personal feelings, likes, interests, dislikes, and such.

A subjective thought is dominated by feelings, preferences, and opinions. It may be an opinion, a rumor, an assumption, a suspicion, or a hunch that is personally influenced from one point of view. Rather than be truth itself, it is an interpretation of truth or reality that presents itself from the angle of the one who is thinking it. It is always at least somewhat biased and will always affect our judgment of people we encounter.

An objective thought is going to be based upon truth and facts. It will not be coloured by past experiences, perceptions, desires, prejudices, opinions formed, or personal feelings. Since the objective thought is entirely based on facts and truth, it can be observed, quantified, and proven to be correct. Since it is completely true without the influence of individual opinion, it is very helpful to use for making rational decisions. It can also be described and imitated.

Here are some examples of objective versus subjective thoughts work:

What is the meaning of the thought?

Objective – Forms a neutral thought which is completely true, unbiased and completely balanced.

Subjective – Forms a thought that does not show a fully clear picture or is only the person's expression of opinion or how they perceive it.

What is the thought based on?

Objective – The thought is based on facts and observations.

Subjective – The thought is based on assumptions, beliefs, or opinions.

Is the thought true?

Objective – The truth behind the thought is 100% provable and true.

Subjective – The truth behind the thought is relative.

Can the thought be verified?

Objective – The thought is completely verified with facts.

Subjective – The thought is open for debate and discussion and not necessarily verified against truth.

From day to day, how is your thought conveyed?

Objective – The thought is conveyed the same every time.

Subjective – The thought varies to a great extent from person to person or day to day.

Sometimes, the differences don't seem completely clear and are a bit confusing to remember. Don't misunderstand. Most of us tend to operate from a subjective mindset. Often, subjective thinking can have some amount of truth or facts in it. But, if it is not 100% verifiable, it is not completely objective.

Remember these key ideas to differentiate between objective and subjective thoughts. An objective thought will be neutral and completely true and real without bias. It will be completely balanced giving you the full picture framed with facts. Whereas, a subjective thought will be framed with your individual outlook or opinion.

An objective thought will be based on facts and careful observation of these facts. Whereas, a subjective thought will rely upon an assumption and will be heavily influenced by personal feelings or emotion.

The information on which we base an objective thought on will be provable, measurable, and observable. Whereas, a subjective thought is relative to the subject at hand.

An objective thought can always be checked out or verified. Whereas, a subjective thought cannot be verified 100%.

When a thought is objective, it will always remain the same regardless of its source, or where you heard or observed it or who reported it to you. Whereas, a subjective thought will change based upon the source and how it is perceived and reported.

An objective thought is appropriate to use for decision making. Whereas, a subjective thought may not be.

Objective thinking is what will produce the absolute truth. It will present thoughts from every angle in a systematic manner. You can rely on objectivity to be factual and proven to be true. Whereas, subjective thinking is going to change and be framed by the character of the person who is thinking it. Subjective thinking interprets or analyses facts based on personal beliefs, perspective, feelings, or opinion.

Though we tend to be wired to be more comfortable thinking one way or the other, it is possible to shift our thinking from subjective to objective by training our thoughts to respond to logical facts that are optimistic in nature. Since objectivity is something you can observe, you will also begin to observe the effect of positive objective thinking in the circumstances around you in real life happenings and events.

What is the science behind this new way of thinking that this 7-day process will reflect a cause and effect in reality?

Laws of Nature

There are many laws by which we live. Some laws govern us, while laws of science are a description of observations. Scientific laws are founded in natural science of physics, chemistry, biology, and earth science that are based on repeated experiments or observations that describe or predict a range of natural phenomena. These laws are developed based upon data collected based on empirical evidence, meaning the information is received by means of observation through the senses and patterns or behaviour are documented through experimentation. The word empirical comes from a Greek word for experience.

The scientific method used to derive laws include a hypothesis, or a guess, to form a pattern in the data you want to understand. This is followed up by collecting data and measuring everything with great precision. Sharing the data and the models with others is another important step, and begins to triangulate the data from every possible aspect. Finally, you evaluate your findings to come to a conclusion.

Laws of science differ from a hypothesis since a hypothesis has not yet been verified. A law also differs from a theory in that it is a distillation of the results of repeated observation and does not try to explain a reason for a phenomena. These laws reflect causal relationships fundamental to reality. In other words, scientific laws sum up the results of experiments and observations. The accuracy of the law will not change with a new theory. For a scientific law to become accepted as a law, it must be true based on observations, universal, simple and expressed with a single mathematical equation, absolute, stable or unchanged, and everything in the universe must comply with them.

Scientific laws can be further developed through mathematics. The mathematics that represent the law does not change. A law can usually be formulated as one or several equations and then be used to predict the outcome of an experiment. To do so, you must first know the circumstances of the processes.

There is a law of magnetism that, in its most basic description, observes that like poles repel one another and unlike poles attract each other. There is also the first law of thermodynamics, also known as the Law of Conservation of Energy, that states energy can neither be created nor destroyed. It can only be transferred or changed from one form to another. For instance, when we flip on a light switch, it may look as though light was producing energy. However, in reality the electrical energy was merely converted. There is also the Law of Vibration that states that everything in the universe moves and vibrates at one speed or another. Nothing rests. But rather, everything you see is vibrating at one frequency or another, including you. The concept is based on the idea that thoughts are energy, so the process of like energy attracts like energy is in line with the Law of Attraction.

Law of Attraction

Using the laws of nature as the base with a bit of knowledge from quantum physics, we can apply these principles to discover that to the way we process our thoughts. The fundamental structures of the world we see, taste, smell, hear, and touch and the world in which we process our thoughts are interwoven. There are patterns in the universe that remain constant and apply to both our physical world and our thoughts. With this in mind, there is a law of attraction that, simply put, states that we attract into our lives whatever we are focusing on. In other words, our thoughts eventually turn into things. If we focus on doom and gloom, we will walk around as if we are under a storm cloud. On the other hand, if we focus on positive thoughts with goals we aim to achieve, we will find a way to achieve them. We act as a human magnet sending out thoughts that attract back to us more of what we have exhibited.

It makes no difference whether or not you agree with these laws or whether or not they make sense to you. The fact remains that there are laws of nature that remain unchanged regardless of whether or not we understand how it works. The exciting part is that these laws of nature can be applied to our thought lives to change physical, real life results within the framework of these laws.

Once we realise this, we are free to take responsibility to begin to change our circumstances by first changing from the cycle of fear, worry, or negativity that has been holding us back all of our lives. It's time to understand how this is done and take the steps necessary to set change in motion to enrich our lives. It all starts with shifting our thoughts from detrimental to productive. The more time you decide to dedicate to understanding the Law of Attraction, the more fulfilling and rich your life will become. These scientific laws do not discriminate as to what kind of person they will work with. The law remains true across the board and across the universe for everyone whether they realise they are applying it to their thought life or not. It is not an attempt to conjure up a distant reality, but rather to focus on what we are thinking and let the law work itself out until we cultivate the end results.

Once we understand the possibilities that lie within Law of Attraction and the huge implications that can manifest by simply changing our thoughts, we see how important it is that we start now to reshape our thoughts to reflect what we hope to attract into our lives. Like a painter with paintbrush ready, begin to change the big picture by selecting what will be represented on that canvas of your life.

With all of this information and proof, begin the 7-day process now

It starts with carefully selecting what thoughts you will begin to dwell upon. What is it that you want to attract into your life? Is it love, is it wealth, is it physical or mental health? Is it a success? Start Increasing your self confidence and combating anxiety right now. Just like an artist carefully crafts their work of art by selecting the paint or the material they will use to reflect what they are hoping to communicate, start changing your thoughts by carefully selecting what ideas you choose to feed your thinking.

Seven Days

This will be the most interesting experiment of all, and it starts with seven days to success. Set aside one week, 7 days, to be your turning point. At the end of this week, nothing will ever be the same again. Begin to change your thoughts by setting aside a week for the sole purpose of establishing new habits of thinking. During these seven days, make it your aim to focus only on shifting your state of mind from negatively damaging to positively mending what is broken in your thought processes.

During this week, the most important thing will be to focus on your thoughts to recondition your state of mind to become more positive in thought, happiness, and balance. The end result will be that you establish a foundation for cause-based thinking instead of effect-based emotional reactions governing your life. By devoting a week to this change you will begin to build a cause-based reality. Instead of merely reacting to what you perceive as reality or allowing others to define these meanings, you will begin to decide what meaning you give to the information and data you receive.

Before you begin: 2-3 days prior

Do not start this week-long process lightly. Give it a lot of thought and consideration. Like training your physical body for a marathon, this will train your mind. It's going to be difficult and at times feel outright exhausting and by no means like a walk in the park. A few days before the seven days begins, you will begin to think very carefully about when you will begin your uninterrupted 7-day project. Seven days may not seem like a long time when you consider that it is usually said to take longer to form a habit. But, the mental work you will undergo during this week is so strenuous that you will not be able to maintain it consciously for longer. Thankfully, a week is all you will need. Give a lot of thought to what is about to happen for a day or two before you begin.

Food for thought

We eat so that we can live and be healthy. The food we put into our body sends nutrients throughout our bloodstream. We can choose to feast on healthy foods or on junk. The same is true with our mental capacity. Only, when it comes to our brains, it is the thoughts we dwell on that becomes our mental food. You've heard the term, food for thought. Well, thoughts really are what feed our thinking. While our physical bodies cannot live very long without food or water, our brains function fed by thoughts. This mental diet is very important.

Replace a negative thought with a positive one, much like when you are on a diet or trying to eat healthier you would replace a nightly snack of crisps with a bowl of celery or an apple. When it comes to food, the choices appear obvious. When it comes to thinking, the substitution process is the same, it's just done inside your brain where no one sees it happening. Substitute the damaging thought with a more productive, healthier option. These thoughts we choose to put into our minds during these seven days are going to be the morsels on which our thinking will feed. Select these thoughts wisely.

Real chemical reaction to words

Words have a biochemical effect on our bodies. Chemical reactions actually change with positive thoughts. As soon as we hear a word like furious, you're going to produce a very different chemical reaction inside your body than if you heard, for instance, "I am a little upset." Likewise, if someone outright calls you a liar, you're going to have a different biochemical reaction that if someone said, "I think you may be mistaken."

This same biochemical response happens with the words we speak to ourselves in our minds. However, we are usually a lot less aware of this impact.

Whether we realise it or not, the words have power. The words we choose to use have an effect on the world around us. People who train customer service representatives know this all too well as the best reps understand that the words can be used masterfully to calm down angry customers. Staying calm and listening goes a long way in diffusing an otherwise volatile situation.

Our thoughts or state of mind are real. They are a causative force in our lives. In fact, we are a collection of these thoughts. Our thoughts are what make up our personality and establish the characteristics of who we are. Based upon these thoughts, we make choices. We choose to go to places that relate to our thoughts.

When we fear something or someone, we give it power. Don't do this. Don't fear, believe the negative or give it power at all. If fear governs us, we move in fear avoiding things that stir up this feeling of fear, not taking a chance on something that might remind us of

that fear, or not going to a place where we a
of this feeling of fear. If expectations of joy, grati
or positive outcomes govern us, our behaviour follows suit and changes to accommodate this. One word of caution is don't mistake these states of mind with an honest gut-level instinct. This is different from a state of fear. The point is that what is reflected in our external world comes about as a result of our thoughts.

Therefore, if we change the way we think, our outward conditions and situations must follow suit and change as well. You choose whether you are in the habit of being sad and dejected or cheerful and upbeat. It all depends upon your thoughts, the way you think, your state of mind.

Chapter Three

AST IS IN YOUR HEAD. FUTURE IS IN YOUR HANDS

Do not dwell on the past

We often blame our negative past experiences for the outcome of our lives, we must not stay there. If we focus on regrets of the past, we will also regret the future. However, if we focus on the positive things, we will have a positive life in front of us. The past is behind us, and we must leave it there in order to move forward into the future. The beauty of it is that when we make the decision to change our thoughts for the better, we open up a door into a more beautiful future of new things we have never encountered before.

If we stay in the past, never allowing ourselves to change our thinking, we will never find out how our story progresses. When we read a book, what would happen if we never turned the page? We would never discover how the story unfolds. We would only know and understand the words we have read up to the point where we placed the bookmark and stopped. Do you want to be stuck in Chapter One for the rest of your life only able to explain or express every experience from the viewpoint of the confines of that page?

Every time we make the decision to open our eyes and put our feet on the floor to begin a new day, we experience new opportunities. The very act of getting out of bed relays hope or a newness of life. If, instead, we choose to think only about things we have experienced in our lives in the past, we cannot move forward. Obviously, if we focus on sad events that we lived through this is the case. But, it is even the case if we choose to hold onto our happy experiences wanting to relive them again and again. Instead, we need to learn to cherish these memories, or come to terms with letting the bad memories go, and take a step forward renewing the way we think.

Stop the negative thought cycle

Elephant trainers used to train the large animals by chaining one of the elephant's legs to a tree. As time went on, the trainer would gradually decrease the size of the chain until it was just a flimsy small string holding the elephant in place. Obviously, a tiny thread could not hold a large elephant in place. The reason the animal would not run off is because he had become accustomed to the original chain. Some even rock back and forth as if they are still chained years after they have been freed. Negative thinking is much like this.

Some people experience negative thinking constantly, and they find it difficult to put out of their heads long enough to progress very far. Some experience this negative thinking because of anxiety or stress which, in turn, heightens the negative thoughts and creates an endless cycle that needs to be broken before thinking can be changed. When you are stressed or anxious, you are more likely to view your circumstances from a negative perspective and think of worst case scenarios that are fearful. We begin to worry about things that haven't even happened yet or think about things that could go wrong. It's a repetition of negativity. These thoughts can happen when we are having a bad day or feeling a bit down. In turn, they make us feel bad about ourselves, we begin to blame ourselves, and point out more negative aspects of our thinking. If these not-so-peaceful thoughts continue, it can lead to sadness and depression. It's very important to catch these cycles and turn them around by changing your thoughts.

Some of the most common negativity cycles of thought include something called mind reading where we automatically think that we know what someone else is thinking, and it's typically not a happy thought. For instance, we may assume someone is ignoring us because they are mad at us.

Another negativity cycle of thought is guilty thinking. This happens when we constantly tell ourselves and dwell upon statements that involve words like should, could, would, or if only. For example, you might tell yourself that you should have gone to workout today which makes you feel guilty for not going to the gym. To combat this negativity cycle, instead acknowledge that the truth is that you didn't go to workout, but then allow yourself the fact that that's OK. Tomorrow is a new day when you can make time to workout. Acknowledge the truth of what happened in a positive way, but don't allow yourself to feel guilty about it. Change the narrative and toss aside those guilty feelings.

Fortune telling is another type of negativity cycle. This is when our minds quickly go to the worst outcome of what could happen. For instance, you have a job interview coming up, but you automatically assume that you are not going to get the job because you'll probably bomb the interview. Stop making these negative predictions on your life. This type of thinking is very destructive since it often leads to low self esteem and giving up, not even trying to succeed.

One of the biggest negativity cycle issues is making comparisons to others with them always coming out on top or better. For instance, you may think someone is so much better looking than you or so much more talented than you. The problem with making a comparison is that when we do this, we no longer realise that everyone has flaws. Begin, instead, to look at your life in a more positive and forgiving light. Remember that other people have difficulties too.

Finally, we stay in a negativity cycle when we play the blame game and blame ourselves or others for mistakes or problems. When we do this, we begin to feel like a failure and can easily spiral negatively out of control. It becomes difficult to view things from a different perspective. Or, you might get in the habit of blaming others and never take responsibility for your own thoughts or actions.

Be kind to yourself, otherwise you will build obstacles to your own success.

State of mind

We have control over what state of mind we choose to dwell in. This is something we must train ourselves to do. It is possible to change this state of how we think. If it were not possible to shift gears in our thoughts, we would really have no control over our life in any way, shape, or fashion. Do not ever accept the idea that you have no control over your emotions. How we respond to our circumstances is what changes our state of mind and the way we think. As our thoughts change, we start to feel better about our circumstances.

Each time we purposely change our thinking from despair to hope, the next time we encounter a circumstance, it becomes easier and easier to change it for the better.

Transmutation is when you turn one meaning into another. We need to do this with negative thoughts, turning them into positive ones. We have the capability of doing this. We can take one emotional response from the world around us and transform it into a completely different emotion. Look at the idea of rejection, for instance. How does it feel when you are rejected? Does it make you feel put down and dejected, or does it empower you? Rejection doesn't have to make us fall into a pit of despair. Instead, we can look at rejection as a chance to become determined to do whatever it takes to overcome it. We can turn the negative impact around into a feeling of excitement and empowerment. The same with criticism. Negative words used to describe our actions can often make us feel low and dejected, or they can be the launching pad to empower us to enter a new state of mind.

What we feel reveals what meaning we have assigned to the things around us, things we experience through our five senses from the external world. Whatever thoughts we choose to accept will change our disposition. What do we interpret as rejection or criticism? It is possible to change this state of mind by changing our thoughts.

First identify the thoughts

Before you can change thoughts from negative to positive, you must first know which thoughts need to be changed. Identify the negative thoughts that happen automatically first. Catch these thoughts and address them before they become a problem. This is more challenging than it might think since these thoughts have become something you are used to. They are automatic, arising without obvious conscious processing. They have become a habit as something you have accepted to be normal. You probably take them for granted and pay very little attention to them. They come into your thinking quickly and leave just as fast.

Some of these negative thoughts crop up based upon specific situations. One way to catch them before they take root is to look for these situations that tend to bring them about. They are usually distorted and repetitive.

Start by recognising your negative thought cycles by keeping a daily record of your thoughts. Jot down any thoughts that make you have a change in your mindset. Immediately ask yourself:

What was going through my mind when I noticed the shift of mindset?

Identify these thoughts and then begin to notice how they kick off a cycle of negativity. From here, you can start to modify the way you think. Begin to generate different ways to think.

There are a few patterns of negative thoughts that are common.

Black and white, all or nothing thinking, also called dichotomous reasoning, is a tendency to look at things as one way or the other and nothing in between. With this way of thinking, there is only black and white and never any shades of grey. People see things as either good or bad, a success or a failure. When, in reality, there is a lot of grey shaded thinking that needs to take place.

Often people jump to conclusions, read minds or tell fortunes, wrongly coming to conclusions about what the person must have been thinking to say or act the way they did. Maybe you were not invited to a party, and you jump to the conclusion that the person must be angry at you.

A binocular trick, or magnification or minimisation is another typical negative thought cycle that we can easily fall into. This is when the negative aspects of a situation become larger than life or magnified while any attempt to seek a positive thought out of the situation is minimised in the scope of things.

Personalising everything is another aspect of negative thinking. You may feel responsible for everything that is out of your control. For instance, you may feel responsible as if it is your fault that someone did not have a good time at your party.

Not giving any credit to the positive is like reversing a beautiful process such as turning a diamond into coal or gold into lead. Any compliment or positive situation is immediately translated into being negative. For instance, you may receive a compliment for a job you did and think that they only complimented you because they want you to do a favour for them.

Over generalising is another way to get stuck in negative thoughts. Words like always or never are prevalent. For instance, you will take a single situation and use it to base your thinking on every other similar situation. You may say that nobody likes you, or they always say bad things about me, or the traffic lights hate me, always turning red and making me late for work.

Making global judgments is labeling something or someone in an unfavorable manner based on a situation. For instance, you may think that someone is an absolute moron.

Should have, could have, would have, ought to, are all words used when you're trapped in moral imperatives. You start to live life according to a set of unbreakable rules that are unattainable and applied to everybody, but usually turned inward to blame yourself for things.

There are also negative thoughts brought about by emotional reasoning where you see the feeling as evidence and proof of the thought itself. For instance, you may say that you feel panicky, and this means that something bad will happen.

Finally, selective abstraction is when you judge the whole on the basis of a small negative aspect. For instance, I completely blew that job interview because I wore the wrong suit.

Identify these patterns, examine them, explore their meanings, and then expose any distortion of thought that is keeping you repeating the negativity. Expand your perspective, and experiment with exchanging the negatives for something better.

Ask yourself:

What evidence do I have that my perception of this situation is correct, what are the implications of my conclusions, and how do I change the thoughts that need to be changed?

As soon as you identify a pattern of negative thinking, begin to ask yourself:

Is there a different way to interpret these facts?

What would be so bad if my knee-jerk perception is correct?

What steps do I take to learn to live with this if that is true?

What are the consequences to believing my initial negative thought?

How do I go about changing or shifting my thinking to get a better result?

Set a timer for 20 minutes. Do not rush the process. Take out a piece of paper and begin to write down these patterns of thought. Make two columns, negative and positive replacements. Under the negative column, write down thoughts that come into your mind as you sit quietly. Once you have several negative thoughts jotted down, begin to evaluate each one and come up with a positive replacement thought for each one. When the 20 minutes has ended, set aside another time to complete another session. Repeat several times.

Do not tell anyone

One of the most important steps to remember during your 7-day thought-enriching experience is to not tell anyone else what you are doing. Keep it a private that only you know about. After you have successfully completed the week long process, allow some time to pass before beginning to talk about it to anyone.

Now, let's begin the seven-day thought-changing process.

Day 1-7

Begin any day of the week and any time of the day. It doesn't matter when you choose to start so long as it continues unbroken for 7 complete days from this point forward. Day one begins with you focusing with a concerted effort on not dwelling on any negative thought. Be very mindful and watchful of yourself not allowing yourself to dwell on any thought that is not constructive, optimistic, uplifting, positive, or kind.

Our 5 Senses determine how we think and perceive our world

Let's start by fully understanding how our brains currently interpret the world around us. Like a computer which runs on data, we receive data through our five senses. Unlike the blind men describing the elephant, however, most of us have five senses from which we perceive and understand our surroundings. These senses are how we interact with the world around us. We taste, see, hear, touch, and smell the things that we encounter so much so that just the scent of a fragrance can trigger a distant memory.

Our five senses include:

1. Seeing
2. Hearing
3. Smelling
4. Tasting
5. Touching

Seeing

Out of all of the senses, our brain devotes more space to processing and storing visual images and perceptions than all of the five senses combined. Unless we are blind, we use our eyes to see. Some of us see with 20/20 perfect vision, while others need glasses or contact lenses to see clearly. Some of us can see fairly well but cannot perceive colour, and are said to be colour blind. So, even though their eyes function to produce sight, they cannot differentiate colours.

The sense of sight is our visual perception or ability to interpret the environment around us using light in the visible spectrum reflected by the objects in the environment. In order for us to see properly, we need several components. The cornea and the lens, transparent structures that are located in front of the eye, focus light onto the retina, which covers almost all of the back of the eye. The shape of our lens actually changes to adjust for near or far vision. When light hits the surface of the photoreceptor, a protein rhodopsin is activated. This begins a series of neurological signals that run along the optic nerve. Their job is to process, sort, and condense these signals. Our brains take this visual input and send it through the visual cortex in the occipital lobe and then to a visual cortex where the data is separated into dorsal pathways to analyse the image size and position. It is also sent to the ventral pathways where it is able to discriminate colour and shape. From the moment we encounter an object to be seen to the instant we see it, more than 30 cortical areas have contributed to this visual processing not to mention the part light and colour plays on the entire process of being able to see.

Hearing

Our ability to hear is a very complex process that requires a series of actions and reactions. Our ears are made up of multiple components, and all of these parts need to work properly together to change sound waves into information that our brains interpret and understand. At birth, a typical ear contains about twelve thousand sensory cells, referred to as hair cells. These hair cells sit on a membrane that vibrates in response to incoming sound. First, the sound waves must enter the ear canal and then travel toward the eardrum causing the eardrum and bones in the middle ear to vibrate. Inside the inner ear, cochlea, there are tiny hair cells which convert vibrations into electrical impulses that the auditory nerve picks up. Each frequency of a sound vibrates the membrane at different locations, so we then hear different pitches within the sounds.

Smelling

Our sense of smell is ten thousand times more sensitive than any other of our senses. Other senses must first travel through neurons and the spinal cord before reaching the brain, but the olfactory response to scents is immediate. This is the only spot where our central nervous system is directly exposed to our environment.

We have a sense of smell to alert us to certain danger, but it is also one of the most powerful in terms of being linked to memory. To be able to smell, a molecule is released from a substance, like the scent of a flower.

This must stimulate the olfactory cells, special nerve cells that are located high inside the nose. These nerve cells then send information to the brain to process the information and identify the scent. The part of our brain that is responsible for our sense of smell is the limbic system, which is also related to feelings and memory. How and why do the sense of smell and the limbic system work together? The sense of smell and the sense of taste are chemical senses since they detect chemicals in our environment. In order for us to process a scent, or vaporised odor molecules known as chemicals must reach our nostrils and dissolve in mucus. Inside the olfactory epithelium, under the mucus, are specialised receptor cells called olfactory receptor neurons which detect odors. These neurons are able to detect thousands of different scents. The olfactory receptor neurons then transmit the information to the olfactory bulb in the back of the nose. The olfactory bulb has sensory receptors that are part of the brain that sends messages to the limbic system and to the neocortex where conscious thought is modified. Our brain perceives the odor, while at the same time, accesses memories associated with the smell.

Tasting

Our sense of smell and taste are related. Our taste consists of a bundle of different sensations. It requires the sense of smell for the sense of taste to determine flavor. Something as simple as a stuffy nose can impair our sense of taste since it affects our sense of smell.

Similar to smell, our sense of taste is also linked to our emotions since both senses are connected to our involuntary nervous system. Scientists have located five basic parts of taste that include sweet, sour, salty, bitter, and savory. What happens through the sense of taste that allows us to perceive flavour is done through a chemical substance which the mouth releases from the taste buds. It activates a nerve cell by changing specific proteins in the wall of the cell. These taste buds are located all around the top of the tongue and are inside various forms of papillae. Adults have between two thousand to four thousand taste buds. The taste buds have several sensory cells, between ten to fifty per sensory cell, that are connected to many different nerve fibers. Eventually, the nerve cells pass information to the brain. While our taste buds receive a great deal of the information, there are actually taste receptors elsewhere inside the mouth, nasal passages, and esophagus. The final part of perceiving taste is to transfer it to the nervous system through several cranial nerves through the medulla oblongata at which some fibers carry taste signals along with signals from other sensory perceptions such as pain, touch, or temperature to our consciousness. Other fibers will pass over other exchange points to produce the possibility of more than one hundred thousand different flavors.

Touching

Touch is the first of our five senses that we develop as a human embryo. In fact, cutaneous tissues and nervous tissues share the same embryological origins. This explains why stress can create a reaction resulting in skin problems. Our skin allows us to have a sense of touch. The skin, through tiny nerve endings, tells our brain information about what it has encountered through a myriad of nerve endings located all over the body. It all starts in the bottom layer of skin known as the dermis. This dermis contains many tiny nerve endings that send information about what we touch to the brain. Our skin contains about twenty different nerve endings that translate whether something is cold, painful, hot, and other information to the brain and spinal cord, or central nervous system. The process of interpreting touch includes sensory receptors that change thermal, mechanical, and chemical energy into electrical signals our brain understands.

There may be more than five senses

As we understand our five senses, there is a new area to explore. Some would argue that we do not have five senses. Or rather, we are not limited to only five senses. Additionally, some argue that we actually possess more senses than the basic five. There are neurologists who suggest we have as many as twenty one senses. There are a couple of additional senses that are an extension of the basic five that include vestibular senses, an awareness of body balance and movement that arises from the inner ear, and proprioception or kinaesthesia senses that arises from muscles, tendons, and joints and have to do with self movement and body position. Regardless, there is evidence that suggests we actually have at least one additional sense from which we gain knowledge, understanding, and new insight about the world around us.

Imagination – our sixth sense

The idea behind changing your thoughts to change the world around us brings in the concept of a sixth sense. This one has to do with imagination and is sometimes referred to as extrasensory perception. With this sixth sense, we subconsciously choose what we want to perceive something even if the five senses deny it. Perhaps, it is our imagination or our dreams that make up this sixth sense. We tend to think of these dreams or imaginations as silliness. We tell children to stop daydreaming and to focus on what is in front of them. We look down on those who seem to be lost in a fantasy land.

But, what if I told you that actually, this sixth sense may very well be our gateway to reality. When we use these imaginations to transform our thinking, we open up a portal for change that generates a cause and effect on the world around us by tapping into the world within our heads.

Use your five senses

We are very familiar with how we interact with the world around us with our five senses. Earlier, we touched upon this. But, did you know you can use these five senses as tools to help you overcome dwelling on negative thoughts? We have the ability to choose our own thoughts and state of mind. We are able to change the meaning attached to these thoughts inside our own minds when we receive data through our five senses and then adjust what this data means.

Studies have revealed that if one of our senses is weak, others will become more active. For instance, blind people often have a heightened sense of smell. Our senses learn to adapt themselves to change and compensate to give us what we need. And, our senses have a huge impact on our behavior. Imagine the aroma of waking up to the smell of a fresh cup of coffee drifting through the air. You can almost taste it as the scent permeates your nose as you breathe. Think about how it feels to hold someone's hand or receive a hug from someone we love. Start with using your sight and your hearing.

Sight - Put your goal in front of you

While your seven-day focus is going to be going on mentally, it helps to have some physical guidance and tools that you will be able to pull out and look at when you need to. One tool that helps is to think about your goals, what you want to achieve by reshaping your thinking. Print this goal, or goals, out on a card that you can pull out and physically look at when you begin to feel weak or begin to waiver. Looking at the goal will remind you of what you are trying to achieve. It will help you keep your focus and move forward. Look at your goals, these are your bulls-eye on the target you are aiming for. Realise that what you are doing during these seven days is contributing to making these goals a reality.

Some find it helpful to make a vision board of sorts that displays goals and thoughts they are trying to attain. If you decide to do this, it doesn't have to be anything elaborate. It can be as simple as writing out some positive words to dwell upon Or, it can be cutting out magazine pictures that help you bring your mind back to these thoughts.

Hearing - Use affirmations

Every impactful speech that inspired action and all of the world's greatest leaders or thinkers have one thing in common. They use words as the power to transform, change emotions, and help inspire others toward their dreams. There is something about speaking and hearing, out loud, the thoughts we are thinking.

If you think about it, you will probably be able to quote some of the most powerful speeches that moved you. Whether it is Winston Churchill's "finest hour" or the "dream" that Martin Luther King, Jr.'s once had, it was the powerful words that moved us to set change in motion, that inspired a move to action and changed the lives of many.

Famous and influential men and women who have shared their words from a platform are not the only ones who can make change happen. How you talk to yourself with your thoughts has a direct influence on how you experience happenings in your life. If your internal speech is negative, you probably encounter negative experiences on a daily basis. If, on the other hand, your internal speech is positive, imagine the change in your circumstances that will occur.

Changing just one word in your self talk will have a major impact on how you feel and how you act. When you change your internal words to be more positive, you will begin to see amazing and fantastic outward experiences change for the better. It is possible to consciously focus on words to use them to improve and change your life for the better.

Researchers from Harvard University along with Google have estimated that the English language has more than a million words, and this number is growing by the thousands each year. Of course, this is taken into account several words that have many forms. In the Oxford English dictionary, there are about six hundred thousand word forms defined. Though, English speakers tend to have a vocabulary between twenty thousand to thirty five thousand words. Skilled authors, like Shakespeare, penned about twenty four thousand words, using five thousand only once in his writings. These words get even fewer as we look at the average English speaker's words are typically only about two thousand and they only habitually use about two to three hundred of these words. When we describe emotions in English, about three thousand words are available, and only one-third of these describe positive emotions.

You decide. What if you could choose how you feel instead of always responding with knee-jerk reactions? The words we attach to our experiences are what become our experiences. Change your words, and you will change your state of mind. When we are proactive in choosing our words that describe our emotions, we can transform an ordinarily angry and upset situation into a more pleasurable one. Begin by setting aside one week where you consciously focus on replacing the negative words you are thinking into more positive ones. Making this shift of emotional patterns and thoughts will begin to shape your decisions, actions, and your entire life circumstances.

Imagine how extraordinary your life could be when you begin to take charge of your emotions simply by changing the thoughts you decide to think. Start lessening the impact of negative emotions so that they no longer have any control over you. Better yet, turn positive experiences into even better ones. Begin small, changing one or two words at a time starting with the negative words that stir up the most powerful negative reactions in you. Change negative words to positive ones, and then go even further beyond to also change positive words to more positive ones, such as changing the word pleased to ecstatic. After seven days of shifting your words, you will have gained a lot of power to change your experiences in life.

Chapter Four
THE POWER OF EXPECTATIONS

Experiment –

The Pygmalion effect

The power of negative and positive thinking can be understood by looking at an experiment that was once conducted by a psychologist named Bob Rosenthal. He wanted to see how long it would take rats to run a maze. He took a group of rats and separated them into cages. He labeled some of the cages, "Maze Bright" and others he labeled "Maze Dull". He then gave the rats inside the labeled cages to a group of students and told them to have the rats run the maze. The results were mouth-droppingly astonishing. The rats that had been labeled as bright finished the experiment with times that were much faster than those who had been labeled as dull. Initially, all of the rats showed no signs of difference in intelligence. The only differing factor was the expectations of those who were running the race. He conducted this experiment several times, with tougher mazes and various groups of people letting the rats run the mazes. He discovered that the rat trainers treated the rats who had been labeled bright differently than those thought to be dull. They would work with the rats thought to be brighter by encouraging them in a different manner than they would the dull rats using different tones in their voice and body language. Over time, the rats responded to the thoughts of expectation whether negative or positive.

This is called the Pygmalion Effect which states that higher expectations lead to an increase in performance. Similarly, the Golem Effect states that lower expectations lead to a decrease in performance.

The idea that someone's expectations of us, or how they convey their thoughts of us, determines our behaviour has also been observed with people. When we lower our expectations of someone, our body language reflects our thoughts. We might stand with more distance away from them or make less eye contact. A teacher's expectation of a student can raise or lower the student's IQ score. A parent can influence their child's behaviour by changing their expectations. Soldiers run faster or slower determined by how their drill sergeant communicates their expectations to them.

Another study was done with teachers and students in a classroom setting. The results found that when teachers were led to expect enhanced performance from the student, then the student's performance was enhanced. Sadly, the opposite was also found to be true for those students whose teachers had a lower expectation of them.

Affirmations

Make a list of affirmations, and read them out loud to yourself often throughout the week. At first, these may feel awkward or even untrue, but as you practice saying them out loud to yourself throughout these seven days, they will become second nature. Exercises are often difficult at first, but the more you practice them and get used to them, the more natural they become.

Sometimes, you may be whispering them quietly under your breath or even merely thinking them to yourself. As long as they begin to shift the way you think for the better, they are doing what they need to do.

Here are several affirmations you can use:

I am a success in everything I do

I keep my focus on what is important

I make the most of every new opportunity

I feel wonderful

I feel alive

I am filled with abundant joy

I speak with confidence

I am healthy

I am happy

I am full of energy

Everything is getting better

I have a calm mind

I am at peace with myself

I am valuable

I matter

I am proud of myself

I feel great

No matter what happens, I know I'll make it

I feel confident

This is super!

I'm luckier than most people

My peers respect me

I have a good sense of humor

I love to laugh

I have a bright future

I'm fun to be with

I am a success

I will be successful

I'm in a great state of mind

There are many people who care about me

I'm pleased with what I have accomplished

I will finish whatever I start

There are many things about me that I like

I have many good qualities

I get along well with others

I am a fortunate person

I have friends who support me

I enjoy a challenge

There is nothing to be afraid of

There is nothing to worry about

I'm very relaxed

I am confident

Everything is going well

I love the way I look

I deserve the very best

I won't give up

My life keeps getting better

Life is exciting!

Thankfulness squashes complaints

People who practice being thankful tend to be happy and easygoing since they always see the positive in even negative situations.

Another way to stir up happiness is to be thankful. Being grateful helps us appreciate what we already have.. Show gratitude toward everything you appreciate. One way to do this is to jot down things you are grateful for, things that make you feel good or boost your state of mind when you are feeling low. Even if it seems like a small or a silly thing, write it down. List five things that you are grateful for.

Some benefits of starting a gratitude journal include lowering stress, feeling calmer and less anxious, gains a new perspective on what is important, get clarity on what you need or want to achieve more of in your life, help you focus on what really matters to you, and helps you learn more about yourself to become more self aware.

Keeping a journal of gratitude is a fantastic way to relax, calm nerves, soothe your mind, and remind yourself daily of the things that really matter. These writings in the journal can help you release bothersome or troubling stuff that messes up your day to day life. Focusing on thankfulness gives you relief from worry and provides you with a purpose or reason to live.

While writing in your journal, be sure to try to reflect thankfulness for things that are happening now. Don't focus too much on the past or on the future. Choose to fill in the journal with a format that is easy and succinct. The shorter and more succinct, the easier it will be to read and remember when you read through it later. Don't limit it to a list format, however, if you feel the need to go more in depth with a bit of an essay format at times.

Your journal is only for you to see, so don't worry about others seeing it. This frees you to be able to express what you really feel and not hold anything back for fear of what someone else will think of what you write down.

On days you feel a bit down, read through the gratitude journal to help adjust your thinking.

It is very helpful to start a gratitude journal. The idea is really easy. You simply write down things that you are thankful for. Start by writing down five things that you have experienced in the past week for which you are grateful. Make sure the entries are brief. A single sentence will do. Don't judge what you include in your gratitude journal. It can be as basic as coffee smelled so good when I awoke Wednesday. Or, it can be sublime or timeless.

The idea is to make yourself become aware of all of the good things in your life. Begin to pay attention to the things around you that brighten up your mindset which we would otherwise take for granted. Look at each entry of thankfulness as a special gift. With each entry, be sure to cherish and savour these gifts.

Why keep a gratitude journal?

Some benefits from journaling include:

Makes you more aware to notice the things that are all around you for which you are grateful for.

Helps you feel more balanced and less distracted by anxiety or stress.

You will begin noticing a lot more small things that are good which are happening.

As you become more thankful, your gratitude will shine on good things and people which will attract even more good things your way to become a circle of thankfulness.

Keeping the journal can make you feel accomplished.

Don't be surprised if you start to become more generous to others.

Journaling can provide a sense of context to remind us how the things in our life are connected to each other.

Focusing on what you are thankful for can help you forgive those in your life who have caused you pain.

Journaling can help you maintain a balanced view of good v. bad things in your life.

It is not a diary where you write every last detail of your daily events, and it is not a daytimer or planner that is intended to schedule your day. A gratitude journal has its own purpose.

Establishing a mindset of gratitude requires more than just simply deciding to be thankful. It will require actively practicing it in order for it to take hold as an attitude of gratitude to become a habit.

The reason it's a powerful exercise to write down things we are thankful for is that it tends to be more powerful than just thinking about what fills us with gratitude. The process of translating our thoughts of gratitude into something you actually see written out makes a huge impact on our mindset. The process of writing allows us to organise our thoughts and own them putting them into context with the world around us.

Don't worry about buying an expensive or overly fancy journal. A spiral notebook is all you need. Though, sometimes decorating your journal or adding a personal touch may help you stay motivated. Feel free to get creative. If you prefer, you can create or find templates which you can download that can be found online. There are also gratitude apps you could use to keep track of your thankfulness. Some even create a ritual around their journal which they look forward to, like lighting a candle, drinking a cup of tea, or taking a hot bath before or while writing in their journal. Feel free to reward yourself every time you write into the journal. The important thing is that you begin to form a habit of noticing and focusing on the things in your life that create gratitude.

Keep these helpful tips in mind as you generate your gratitude journal.

Be motivated to become happier through journaling about what you are thankful for. Make a conscious decision to become happier and more grateful. Don't just go through the motions of writing down something to fill the pages. Really search yourself to discover what makes you happy and thankful.

Go into detail as often as possible. Elaborating the details on the items you are helpful for is much better than just a mere list of items.

Personalise it by zooming in on people you are grateful for. When you focus on the people who you are happy to be in your life, it holds more weight than when you list things you are grateful for.

Take away. Instead of just racking up a long list, imagine what your life would be like without specific things or people.

Surprise! Write down everything that happened that you did not expect but that made you happy. Surprises bring about strong emotions and feelings of thankfulness.

Don't get burnt out. Write a few things down every other day, or even once or twice a week. Don't overdo filling out the pages to burn out.

Start by writing down things you are grateful for such as:

Your health

Family members

You sense of sight

Your friends

Refreshing rain

Happy memories

Your work

Your pet

Your education

The sound of the sea

The sound of birds chirping

If you need some ideas to get started keeping a gratitude journal, follow these writing prompts:

Jot down four silly things your kids did today.

What are three ways to say thank you to someone?

Write a thank you note to yourself.

What are you thankful for that makes you unique?

Look outside. What is the first thing you see that makes you grateful?

If you had to give up everything you own but could keep three things, what three things would you hold onto and why?

Write down five small ways that you can share thankfulness today.

List 7 things you are grateful for as a co-worker.

List 5 things that make you thankful as a mom.

List 10 things that make you grateful for as an adult.

Describe a person in your life whom you are thankful for, and explain why.

List skills or talents you are grateful that you have.

Choose a random picture, and write about it. What makes you grateful about this memory?

Think about something that is difficult or challenging right now. Look for something in the challenge that you are grateful for.

What activities or hobbies would you miss if you couldn't do them?

How is your life different today, in a positive way, compared to a year ago?

Write down five body parts that you are thankful for and why these make you gracious.

Write about something you are looking forward to.

List three things that made you crack a smile this week.

Name someone who did something nice for you without being asked.

Write about something great in your life today that you didn't have a year ago.

Reflect on a time you learned something from a mistake you made.

What do you like about your house?

Write about someone who helped turn you into the person you are today and what this means to you.

Think about a time when you were able to help someone other than yourself.

Write about a person you haven't spoken with in a while.

Write about a musician, an author, or an artist whose work inspired you.

Think about your morning coffee.

Write about your favorite food.

List three people who helped you through a rough time.

What are you taking for granted about your days that you are thankful for when you think about it.

List five people in your life that you have trouble getting along with, including at least one quality you appreciate about each one.

Write about the city where you live.

Write about a nearby park.

Write about your bed.

Talk about your hometown.

Write about a family tradition you enjoy.

Jot down a silly moment.

Talk about a recent change in our life and what made you happy about it.

Write about a recent accomplishment.

Write about the seasons of the year and what you like about them.

What aspects of your work setting do you like?

When was the last time you had a good laugh, what triggered it?

What have you learned this week that you are happy to know?

Write a letter to someone who has changed your life in a positive manner.

What part of your morning routine are you most gracious for?

What part of nature are you thankful for and why?

What foods do you like?

Who has done something this week to help you, and how can you thank them for this?

Write about the music you enjoy.

What one material item are you most thankful for?

Keep your journal on your bedside cabinet and make a plan to write something in your journal for 15 minutes before you get into bed. Set a timer. If morning works better for you, do it then. Don't worry about how deep or detailed your journal is. It's OK to keep it simple. Be sure to treat yourself with kindness, and when things seem to be going wrong, allow yourself time to step away to focus on what is going right. Remember that thankfulness is about becoming aware of what you already have and not to focus on what you don't have. The more you focus on thankfulness, the easier it will be to come up with more grateful things to focus on.

Chapter Five
YOU REAP WHAT YOU SOW

Impression and expression and the subconscious mind

There is much talk in the psychological realm about how our minds work and how much the subconscious mind controls our thoughts and actions. Whether or not you believe that we have a subconscious or embrace or deny its potential, the fact is that there is evidence it not only exists but has a lot of power to change the way we perceive the world around us. One of the most powerful skills you can ever learn in life are those that contribute to establishing balance in your life. To do this, we must adjust to bring into balance the information that is given to use every day through our five senses so we can impress it upon our subconscious mind and then express it outwardly. Once we express it outwardly, it further emphasises and impresses all the more on our subconscious mind. You are not conjuring up make believe, but rather establishing your outward reality from that which originated within your subconscious. In the end, this process creates a new reality.

Your conscious mind has the responsibility of guarding what is allowed into your subconscious. It is a guard set up to protect your thinking from false impressions. Whatever your conscious mind assumes or trusts to be true is what your subconscious mind will accept as truth as well. You are in charge of this thought process. You are the captain or the navigator who will direct your mind to proper thinking.

The subconscious is the world within. When there is balance within, it will be reflected in the outward world.

What thoughts are negative?

Failure, disappointment, trouble, spite, condemning of others, sickness, accident, limitation, fear-based or pessimistic thinking. All of this is limited thinking. There is so much more to life. There is another side to things.

What is negative thinking?

Negative thinking is any thought or failure, disappointment, criticism, trouble, spite, condemnation of yourself or of others, sickness, jealousy, pessimistic, anything that is not positive or constructive in character in regards to you personally or for someone else, or limitations you choose to entertain and accept as thoughts.

Some of the most common negative thoughts we will encounter will be:

I don't have enough time

I am so inadequate

Nobody cares about me

I don't know what I'm doing

I am a failure

The world is a horrible place

Instead of saying I always make mistakes, say I do many things well.

Instead of saying I am stupid, say I am smart.

Instead of saying what a jerk or unpleasant person I am, say I am a wonderful person

Instead of saying I don't deserve a good life, say I deserve to be happy and healthy.

Instead of saying I feel like I'm up against the world, say I have friends who support and love me

Instead of saying I'm no good, say I am amazing

Instead of saying no one understands me, say I am unique and empathetic of others

Instead of saying I don't think I can go on, say, I will take a deep breath, get some rest and keep going

Instead of saying I'm so weak, say I am getting stronger every day.

Instead of saying I'm so disappointed in myself, say tomorrow is a new day where I can improve.

Instead of saying I hate myself, say I love myself.

Instead of saying I'm worthless, say, I'm valuable.

Instead of saying I'm a failure, say I'm a success.

Instead of saying It's just not worth it, say anything worth doing is worth the effort and hard work.

Instead of saying I feel so helpless, say I will reach out to help someone today.

Instead of saying I don't have enough time, say I will reorganise my day for things that matter to me.

Instead of saying I am so inadequate, say I have the skills needed to get the job done.

Instead of saying nobody cares about me, say I have compassion for others.

Instead of saying I don't know what I'm doing, say I am learning new things.

Instead of saying the world is a horrible place, say I will make the world a brighter place with my smile

Instead of saying I'm a loser, say I will focus on what I am good at

Instead of saying why can't I ever succeed, say I am a success

Instead of saying I've let people down, say I will repair broken relationships

Instead of saying I wish I were a better person, say I am improving every day.

Instead of saying My life's not going well, say I am taking steps to make my life better

Instead of saying Nothing feels good anymore, look for positive bright spots

Instead of saying What's wrong with me, say what is right about me?

Instead of saying I wish I could just disappear, say whose life can I enrich today?

Instead of saying My life is a mess, look for what is right about it

Instead of saying I'll never make it, say, I will never give up.

Instead of saying There must be something wrong with me, look at your good points

Instead of saying I will never add up to anything, say only I can change the way I view my future.

Let a thesaurus be your best friend

A thesaurus is like a dictionary, only it lists words and gives us words that mean the same thing that we can use instead of those words. Though, it does one additional helpful thing as well. It also lists out antonyms, or opposite words for every word in the thesaurus. This is where picking up a thesaurus can really begin to turn your life around. Turn your negative thoughts into positive ones.

Some examples of positive thoughts and emotions to focus on include:

- Accepted admiring adoring affection amazed amusement assured attentive
- Beaming beautiful blissful brilliant
- Calm carefree celebrated charming confident contentment courageous
- creative
- Dazzling delighted determined distinguished
- Ease ecstatic effective effervescent efficient empathetic engaged energetic
- enthusiastic electrifying encouraging energetic enthusiastic essential
- esteemed excellent excited exquisite
- Fabulous fantastic flourishing fortunate free friendly fulfilled
- Generous genius genuine giving glowing good gorgeous graceful
- great glad good grateful
- Happy harmonious healthy honest honorable hopeful
- Ideal impressive innocent inspired intelligent interested

- Jolly jovial joy jubilant
- Kind
- Laughter lovely loving
- Marvelous masterful meaningful motivated
- Optimistic
- Passionate peaceful perfect phenomenal pleasant pleased pleasure
- poised polished positively powerful productive
- Quality
- Refreshing rejoice reliable remarkable resounding respected restored
- relieved respected
- Satisfied self-collected serenity skilled smile sparkling special stupendous
- successful super
- Tender terrific thoughtful triumphant trust
- Upbeat upstanding
- Valued vibrant
- Wonderful worth wow
- Yes
- Zealous

Try to rid your entire vocabulary and thought life of even the hint of negativity. A word becomes negative when it shows rejection or disagreement or judgment imposed. When you identify that you are thinking a negative thought, make every effort to immediately turn your thinking around to instead dwell on the opposite of your initial negativity. Flip your thoughts around. It's going to require a conscious effort to make the change in your thinking. Some clues that a word should be replaced in our thinking is if it starts or ends with "un", "im", "in", "irr", "mis", "dis", "non", "de", "mal", "less", "anti", "counter", or "phobic!" Also, replace words like never or no. All of these words that begin or end with negative connotations can be switched with those that imply a more favorable way of saying it. For example:

Negative	**Positive**
disagreeable	agreeable
Disrespectful	respectful
Inconsistent	consistent
Maladjusted	adjusted
Malnourished	nourished
irrational	rational
irreconcilable	reconcilable

irregular	regular
irresistible	resistible
immobile	mobile
immoral	moral
imperfect	perfect
impossible	possible
impolite	polite
impatient	patient
impure	pure
improbable	probable
inaccurate	accurate
ineligible	eligible
indecent	decent
incompetent	competent
incapable	capable
incorrect	correct
incompatible	compatible
unhappy	happy
unable	able
uninteresting	interesting

uncomfortable	comfortable
unhelpful	helpful
unprepared	prepared
unhealthy	healthy
unfair	fair
unfriendly	friendly
antisocial	social

It helps to have information in front of us to help guide us through the process. Start by swapping out the actual words you've become accustomed to thinking with happier, more balanced ones, such as on the chart below which has been put in alphabetical order to make it easier to locate the negative thought quickly. As soon as you think it, you will be able to find the negative word and locate the opposite, positive replacement:

Negative Thought	Instead Think these Positive Thoughts
abandoned	welcomed, adopted, supported, cherished, defended
abysmal	superb, admirable, breathtaking, stunning, magnificent
adverse	advantageous, helpful, favorable, fortunate, beneficial
afraid	fearless, undaunted, brave, bold, heroic

aggressive calm, easy-going, peaceful, harmonious, serene

alarming comforting, reassuring, consoling, soothing, calming

angry happy, cheerful, peaceful, pleased, joyful, content

annoyed pleased, appreciative, happy, satisfied, content

antagonistic agreeable, friendly, kind, nice

anxious courageous, unafraid, assured, tranquil, calm, confident

apathetic compassionate, concerned, interested, responsive, caring

appalling attractive, beautiful, nice, delightful, pleasant, good

apprehensive confident, at ease, certain, clear, composed

arrogant thoughtful, humble

ashamed confident, bold, joyful, happy, glad

astonished expectant, elated

atrocious magnificent, good, wonderful, inoffensive

awful delightful, wonderful, nice, great, OK

bad good, reputable, worthy, upright, right

banal intelligent, new, original, smart, uncommon, fresh

barbed mild, nice, complimentary, flattering

belligerent peaceful, friendly, kind, cooperative, helping, nice

bemoan happiness, celebrate, rejoice, triumph

beneath above, higher, on top of

betrayed faithful, loyal, defend, support, aid, help, assist bitter sweet, genial, kind, pleasant, nice

blame approve, harmony, health, peace, sanction, thanks

bored interested, excited, energised, refreshed, enthusiastic

boring interesting, fascinating, new

broken fixed, complete, uplifted, whole

callous mindful, tender, compassionate, caring, nice

can't can, determined, fortitude, goal-minded, press on

cautious sure, confident, let your guard down, certain

clumsy agile, graceful, coordinated, expert, athletic

coarse refined, smooth, gentle, delicate, nice, clean, polished

cold warm, friendly, attentive, interested, responsive

cold-hearted caring, compassionate, friendly, kind, involved

collapse build up, standing strong, increase, rise, success

confused understood, orderly, organised, composed, clear

contemptuous respected, lovely, approachable, friendly

contradictory encouraged, balanced, consistent, reconcilable

contrary harmonious, agreeable, consistent, friendly, kind

corrosive contributing, gentle, fortifying, supporting, nice

corrupt ethical, good, honest, honorable, respectable, trustworthy

crazy balanced, in your right mind, rational, sane, believable

creepy pleasing, good, nice, pleasant

criminal legitimate, legal, right, uncorrupted, authorised, blessed

critical complimentary, praising, treasure, admirable, applauded

cruel kind, compassionate, considerate, humane, merciful

cry laugh, smile, happy, quieted, peaceful, content, comforted

cutting gentle, kind, nice, soothing, sweet, pleasant

cynical believing, hopeful, optimistic, trusting, undoubting

damage built up, constructed, improved, healed, repaired

damaging helpful, favorable, beneficial, advantageous

dastardly honorable, respectable, worthy

dead alive, active, enduring, unfinished

decaying growing, improving, increasing, rising, flourishing

deformed whole, beautiful, free, untwisted

demure brave, strong, outgoing

deny accept, approve, support, acknowledge, embrace

deplorable respectable, successful, excellent, fortunate, good

depressed unburdened, flourishing, prosperous, encouraged, cheerful

deprived privileged, rich, prosperous, wealthy

despair hope, joy, encouragement, happiness, peace, confidence

despicable honorable, respectable, reputable, lovable, virtuous, nice

detestable admirable, adorable, cherished, likeable, prized, respected

detrimental assisting, favorable, helpful, positive, beneficial

dirty clean, bright, neat, orderly, tidy, spotless, upright, pure

disappointed satisfied, pleased, heartened, happy, fulfilled, delighted

disapproving accepted, approved, welcomed, liked, commended

discontented contented, pleased, satisfied, happy

disease health, soundness, strength

disgusting beautiful, magnificent, desirous, pleasing

disheveled orderly, organised, together

dishonest truthful, valid, reliable, genuine, ethical, above-board

dishonorable blameless, principled, respectable, trustworthy

disillusioned encouraged, see the truth, happy, fulfilled, satisfied

dismal bright, cheerful, clear, encouraging, joyful, light

dismayed enlightened, pleased, reassured, comforted, delighted

dismissive thoughtful, attentive, caring

disrespectful courteous, respectful, polite, mannered, nice

distant close by, approachable, friendly, kind, neighborly, warm

distress calm, peaceful, joyous, helped, delighted, cheered

don't allow, approve, permission, do

down/down in the dumps rise above, cheerful, happy, heartened, lifted up

drained filled, energised, lively, energetic, satisfied

dreadful beautiful, pleasant, welcomed, wonderful, delightful

dreary sunny, bright, cheerful, colourful, exciting, glad, hopeful

embarrassed composed, confident, happy, self worth

empty full, satisfied, sufficient, fruitful, overflowing

enraged joyous, calm, happy, cheerful, pleased

envious confident, comfortable, content, pleased, kind

eroding built up, preserved, constructed, rebuilt, fixed

evil good, whole, right, virtuous, moral, auspicious

exasperated refreshed, delighted, helped, pleased, soothed, tranquil excluded included, accepted, welcomed, chosen, approved, support

exhausted invigorated, refreshed, energised, restored, plenty, strong

fail succeed, accomplish, achieve, gain, prosper, reach

fatigued energetic, fresh, invigorated, vivacious, alert

faulty faultless, flawless, honest, sufficient, unbroken

fear faith, assurance, confidence, comfort, brave, calm

feeble capable, competent, efficient, fit, strong, unbreakable

fidgety restful, relaxed, composed, calm, easy-going

fight peaceful, friendly, kind, harmonious, balanced

foul pleasant, perfect, good

fragile strong, able, healthy, durable, unbreakable

frightened courageous, calm, unafraid, happy, cool, brave

frightful pleasant, delightful, wonderful, gentle, beautiful

frustrated encouraged, fulfilled, uplifted

furious cheerful, happy, elated, peaceful, gentle

gawky graceful, artful, dexterous, move with ease, skillful, handy

ghastly delightful, beautiful, wonderful, pleasant

gloomy vivacious, sparkling, exhilarating, sunny, hopeful

grave life, cheerful, happy

greed generous, benevolence

grief cheer, comfort, relief, peace, joy, happiness, hope

grim hopeful, encouraging, wonderful, joyful

grimace grin, smile, happy countenance, pleasant disposition

gross or grotesque pretty, nice, beautiful

gruesome attractive, beautiful, cheerful, delightful, pleasing

grumpy/grouchy thankful, cheerful, happy, nice, pleasant

guilty innocent, truthful, good, right, immune

haggardcolourful, fresh, hearty, strong, healthy

hapless happy, fortuitous, fortunate, well-off, lucky

hard delicate, flexible, merciful, nice, sympathetic, easy

hard-hearted gentle, amenable, kind, thoughtful, empathetic

harmful helpful, favorable, beneficial, profitable, safe

hate love, good will, kind, like, regard, admire, respect, esteem

heart-broken lighthearted, pleased, happy, enriched, fulfilled

helpless able, strong, confident, enterprising, resourceful, skilled

hesitant brave, decisive, eager, fearless, ready, sure, willing

hideous charming, wonderful, pleasing, likeable, delightful

homely attractive, beautiful, becoming, lovely

hopeless promising, propitious, rosy, auspicious, expectant

horrendous delightful, wonderful, pleasant, nice, beautiful, good

horrible magnificent, soothing, reputable, calming, comforting

horrified delighted, calm, unafraid, courageous, happy

hostile welcoming, warm, kind, hospitable, favorable, friendly

humiliated honored, favorable, restored

hurt healed, repaired, healthy, cured, remedied, well

hurtful helpful, relieving, safe, beneficial, assisting, aiding

icky nice, pleasing, desirous, clean, magnificent

idiotic wise, intelligent, thoughtful, smart, reasonable, sane

ignorant knowledgeable, aware, talented, wise, intelligent

ignore acknowledge, notice, recognise, succeed, take note

ill well, healthy, strong, good, sound

immature mature, experienced, grown, developed

impatient patient, enduring, forbearing, laid-back

imperfect perfect, complete, faultless, unflawed, pure, unblemished

impossible possible, obtainable, achievable, hopeful

inadequate abundant, sufficient, more than enough

inane smart, intelligent, bright

indignant peaceful, calm, cheerful, gleeful, pleased, happy

indifferent sympathetic, involved, interested, compassionate

inelegant elegant, glamorous, graceful, sophisticated, refined

infernal angelic, heavenly, moral

inferior superior, important, necessary, best, extraordinary

infuriated peaceful, care-free, happy, pleased, calm, cheerful, joyous

injure protect, fix, heal, improve, help, assist, cure, strengthen

insane balanced, sane, rational, intelligent, reasonable

insecure secure, protected, safe, confident, unafraid, peaceful

insidious honest, fair, sincere, open

insignificant important, meaningful, relevant, significant, valuable

insipid appetising, exhilarating, exciting, interesting, original

isolated included, cherished

insulted complemented, flattered, praised, encouraged, valued irate calm, pleased, happy, cheerful

incensed joyous, cheerful, pleased, happy

jealous trusting, confident, satisfied, undoubting

jittery relaxed, unworried, laid-back, easy-going, composed

judgmental accepted, welcomed, loved

junky nice, refined, sophistical, neat, tidy, valuable, enriched

kill life, enrich, build up, give birth, loose, save, construct

knock compliment, praise, treat well, help, assist, protect

knotted free, straight, untwisted, loosed

kook sane, clever, whole, accepted, loved, unique

let downencouraged, satisfied, benefited

livid rosy, radiant, happy, cheerful, brilliant

lonely cherished, valued, welcomed, loved, support

lose find, keep, succeed, hold on to, achieve, accumulate

lousy worthy, magnificent, nice

mad happy, of sound mind, cheered, rational, balanced

malicious assisting, forgiving, friendly, thoughtful, benevolent

mean kind, generous, compassionate, noble, nice, polite

melancholy cheerful, happy, joyful, sunny, heartened

menacing helping, assisting, lending a hand, building up

messy neat, uncluttered, clean, systematic, organised, orderly

misery boon, benefit, advantage, hopefulness, relief, happiness moan compliment, praise, shouts of joy, relief

moldy new, fresh, clean

monstrous natural, magnificent, pleasing, inoffensive, becoming

naive aware, knowledgeable, wise, experienced, intelligent

nasty pleasant, decent, magnificent, nice, delightful

naughty nice, pure, moral, respectable, admirable

nauseated hearty appetite, healthy, well, happy, satisfied

negate approve, uphold, support, confirm, validate, permit, prove

negative positive, affirmative, favorable, confident, good

nervous calm, assured, confident, relaxed, bold, brave

never always, forever, attainable, achievable, constant

no yes, favorable, affirmative, approval

nobody somebody, important, valued, famous, loved

nondescript superior, remarkable, illustrative, distinguished

nonsense wisdom, intelligibility, understanding, sense, possessions

not possible, attainable, achievable

noxious wholesome, pure, curing, sweet, kind, helpful

numb sympathetic, compassionate, responsive

objectionable delightful, kind, pleasant, pleasing, welcoming

obstinate helpful, willing, flexible, amenable

odious attractive, delightful, kind, likeable, lovable, pleasant

offensive delightful, pleasant, respectful

old new, fresh, youthful, recent, up-to-date

oppressive freeing, unburdensome, uplifting

out of control orderly, manageable, organised

overwhelmed manageable, under control, in charge, encouraged, win

pain relief, soothe, help, heal, fix, assist, assuage, alleviate

panic calm, relaxed, confident, content

perplexed certain, clear, sure

persecuted lifted up, rewarded, freed, soothed, commended

perturb assist, assure, calm, clear up, enlighten, reassure

pessimistic encouraging, optimistic, trusting, confident, sunny

petty significant, first-class, first-rate, important, prominent

plain unique, extraordinary, dressed-up, beautiful, attractive

poisonous non-toxic, benevolent, wholesome, life-giving

poor rich, affluent, full, wealthy, fertile, superior, strong

powerless powerful, able, capable, competent, effective, potent

prejudice impartial, fair, approval, respect, admiration, love

pressured eased, relief, release

provoked at ease, forgiving, loving

prudish brave, bold, friendly

questionable assured, certain, proven, trustworthy, definite

quirky unique, genuine, one-of-a-kind, valuable

quit begin, start, fresh, persevere, complete, arrive, continue rage peace, calm, happy, complement, flatter, praise, soothed

regretful content, happy, not guilty, satisfied

rejected cherished, accepted, welcomed, approved

remorseful joyful, happy, glad

repelled attract, accept, approve, increase

repugnant likeable, pleasing, friendly, nice, delightful

repulsive wonderful, inviting, delightful, friendly, attractive

resentful forgiving, helpful, pleasant, kind

restless easy-going, relaxed, settled, laid-back, composed, content

revenge pardon, forgive, sympathy

revolting pleasing, delightful, nice, lovable, comforting

ridiculed approved, compliment, flatter, praise

rocky smooth, dependable, steady

rotten good, fresh, helpful, perfumed, sweet

rude nice, polite, sophisticated, mannerly, respectful

rushed relaxed, in control

ruthless giving, considerate, tender, humane, compassionate

sad happy, cheerful, glad, joyful

savage sophisticated, refined, polished, cultured, nonviolent

scary soothing, comforting, encouraging, calming

self-conscious self-confident, bold, friendly

shame respect, approval, esteem, honor

sheepish bold, confident

shocked elated

shoddy respectable, noble, refined, sophisticated superior

sick healthy, perfect, sound, strong, well

sickening delightful, pleasing, healthy, nice

sinister benevolent, kind, nice, auspicious, happy

skepticalundoubting, certain, convinced, definite, trustworthy

sleepy alert, lively, energetic

slimy smooth, clean, fresh

smelly Fragrant, aromatic, pleasant

sneaky forthright, aboveboard, trustworthy, honest

sobbing cheering, shouts of joy, laughter, gleeful

sorry glad, heartened, nice, hopeful, happy, joyful

spiteful friendly, forgiving, loving, affectionate, lovable

startled at rest, peaceful, calmed, unafraid

stinky fragrant, pleasant, aromatic

stormy peaceful, calmed, clear, gentle

stressful at ease, peaceful, calm, comforted

stuck free, released

stupid smart, intelligent, cognizant, wise, thoughtful, sensible

substandard above average, quality, magnificent

sullen cheerful, friendly, gentle, happy, joyful, grinning

sulky cheerful, happy

suspicious trustworthy, palpable, innocent, sure, certain

sufferingrelief, joy, happiness, favor, ease, advantage

suspect innocent, known, trusted

suspicious certain, confident, convinced, sure, trusting

tense relaxed, calm, flexible

terrible wonderful, delightful, pleasant, amazing

terrified peaceful, assured, comforted

threatened safe, protected

tired invigorated, well rested, energised, refreshed, fresh

ugly beautiful, lovely, pleasant, easy on the eyes, attractive

undermine support, strengthen, relieve, encourage, help, fix, construct

uneasy at ease, sure, confident, brave, peaceful, unworried

unfair fair, just, unbiased, justifiable, impartial, ethical

unfavorable favorable, advantageous, fortunate, positive

unfocused focused, clarified, clear, attentive

unhappyhappy, cheerful, giddy, joyful, happy, elated

unhealthy healthy, well, strong

unjust just, fair, impartial, unprejudiced, equitable, unbiased

unlucky lucky, fortunate

unpleasant pleasant, delightful, nice, kind, helpful, friendly

unsatisfactory satisfactory, pleasing, acceptable, sufficient

unsettled settled, established, certain, stable, composed

unsightly attractive, pleasing, pretty, sightly, nice, beautiful

unsure sure, confident, steadfast, secure, trustworthy

untoward fortunate, happy, lucky, acceptable, auspicious

unwanted wanted, valued, cherished, accepted, desired

unwelcome welcome, accepted, wanted, desirable

unwholesome wholesome, healthful, nutritious, proper,seemly

unwieldyhandy, light, helpful, graceful, coordinated, agile

unwise wise, sagacious, responsible, thoughtful, sensible

upset undisturbed, settled, happy, confident

vice improved, strong, growth, developed

vicious friendly, tame, nice, gentle, civilised, pleasant

victimised protected, assisted, helped

vile pure, worthy, virtuous, safe, desirous

villainous heroic, respectable, honorable, nice, helpful

vindictive compassionate, considerate, forgiving, giving

violated purified, regarded, helped, assisted

vulnerable protected, strong, secure, safe

weak strong, able, hearty, powerful, stable, steady, capable

weary energetic, energised, invigorated, refreshed

wicked angelic, good, honest, moral, upright, honest, proper

withdrawn known, confident, visible, acknowledged

woeful cheerful, encouraging, glad, worthwhile, wealthy, rich

worried assured, undisturbed, untroubled, relaxed, comforted

worthless valuable, beneficial, meaningful, useful, significant

wound heal, help, comfort

yell kind, gentle, tender

yucky delightful, pleasant, nice, clean

zero something, somebody, very important, more than enough

Everyone will begin on a different level. Sometimes, it helps to start slow. For instance, if you are furious, out of your mind livid with a situation, you may not be at the point where you can turn that around to a more positive, rosy thought. So, start by replacing livid, furious, or out of your mind and mad with the word "miffed". Listen to how much less severe your thoughts suddenly sound when instead of saying, "I'm livid!" You, instead say, "I'm miffed."

Chapter Six

DANCE TO YOUR OWN TUNE

Also change your tone

Sometimes it's not just the words we speak but the tone in which we speak them that impacts our lives. Think for a moment the difference of the impact of how the words, "I love you!" is spoken. Imagine it is spoken in an angry tone, a joking tone, or a sneering tone. All of those hold very different meanings than the tender, sweet, heartfelt sentiment these words usually imply.

Sound waves are a mechanical wave that is produced by the back and forth vibration of particles. When sound waves hit the eardrum, they cause it to vibrate. These vibrations are then transferred through three small bones inside the ear into the cochlea. Vibrations in the cochlea are transformed into electrical signals that our brains interpret as sound. We hear different sound pitches, high or low, based on the sound wave's frequency. The higher the frequency, the higher the pitch. When we increase the volume of the tone, we add energy to the sound wave. The result is more vibrations. With sound waves, a large enough vibration could knock objects off of a table with the eventual movements. But, there is something else that happens. If you sprinkle sugar or salt granules on wax paper and then create a series of vibrations, you will notice that the granules move in different patterns depending on the frequency of the tone. With this in mind, think about how the tone we use in our speech changes the way we interpret the words.

The entire process will be easier if you do some basic things that may even sound a bit silly at first. These include:

Smile

Gather positive people around you

Take responsibility

Offer your help to someone

Sing

When we smile, we actually lift our countenance and tone of voice. I'm sure you're heard all of the physical explanations of how smiling requires less muscle work than frowning. So, if it's so much easier to smile than to frown or snarl, why is it so hard to train ourselves to do it?

Smile

When receptionists are trained to answer the phone for a company, they are often sent to seminars to teach them how exactly to pick up the phone and talk. The first rule of thumb is to always smile as you're answering and greeting the caller. Even if you never answer a phone with a smile, do one experiment. Smile, and look in the mirror. Now, frown. Finally, just give a blank, plain look. Which one do you prefer? If you were to meet you for the first time, wouldn't it be more welcoming and open the door to accepting you for who you are if you simply smile? It's such an easy experiment to try. All you have to do is practice smiling?

Gather positive people around you

We all have that one person in our lives who knows how to bring us down no matter how happy we feel. Whether we realise it or not, we also know people in our lives who consistently make us feel good. These positive friends are the ones you want to gather around you to give you support while you're trying to retrain your thinking. Gathering positive people around us is very important. You don't have to throw a party every night, but guard your contacts like a hawk, only allowing those to rally around you who have proven to be those who perk you up.

Take responsibility

Gathering people around us who have a positive effect on us is important, but ultimately the actual changes that take place will be our own responsibility. Changing the way you think and anticipating your circumstances to change as a result is going to be up to you. You are the only one who is responsible for changing the way you think.

Offer your help to someone

This week-long exercise is going to take a lot of concerted work on your part. So, anything that eases the stress of it all is important. One sure-fire way to ease stress is to reach out, take your focus off of yourself for a while, and help someone else. Do something nice for another person.

Sing

It doesn't matter if you are musically inclined or if you've never sung a note in your life. Singing makes us feel better. When we sing, we express emotion that relieves stress. When we sing, there are physiological things that happen to our body. Singing releases endorphins which makes us feel good. When we sing in front of a crowd, even if it's just for fun with a karaoke night, it builds confidence. Some studies have shown that singing decreases anxiety and depression and lifts our outlook on life. Singing has the same uplifting feeling on us as exercise. It provides an aerobic activity that delivers more oxygen throughout our body. It necessitates deep breathing which reduces anxiety. For starters, try singing some affirmations to yourself.

Read positive quotes

Seek out literature and articles that provide a positive outlook. When you come across a positive quote, write them down and put them in front of you so you can read them time and time again as you go through the

7-day adventure. Remember that your thoughts become words, your words become actions, your actions become habits, your habits become character, and your character becomes your future.

Meditating on good thoughts requires training yourself to do so. The process will change the tone of our thoughts from negative to positive, and will in turn change our circumstances and everything around us. To do this successfully, you must remember that no one is perfect. Allow yourself some leeway and grace to move forward. Don't dwell on your mistakes that you have made in the past or whether or not you've tried the 7-day exercise and failed to complete it the first time. The only thing left to do now is to learn from your mistakes and take one step in front of the other to move forward.

Our diet

If you look at it as if you are putting your mind on a diet, it is a helpful imagery to keep you going. Think of your thoughts as if they are food for your brain. One nutrition campaign years ago had a slogan that said, "You are what you eat." What this meant was that the food we eat sends nutrients throughout our bloodstream and builds our bodies or tears our bodies down depending on what we feed it. If the saying is true that "You are what you eat," then how much more will it be true that we become what we think about.

As you feed your mind better, healthier thoughts, it will change for the better. In turn, your circumstances will also change. How much more important is it to feed our minds the proper thoughts. Everything in your life is perceived by the thoughts and feelings you have about them. Your future will be framed by the thoughts and feelings you have today. Whether you are happy or fearful will depend upon what thoughts we feed our mind. You cannot be happy with wrong thoughts. Start feeding your mind healthy morsels by turning negative thoughts into positive ones.

7-day life-changing diet plan

When we hear diet plans advertised as being the best plan for you, the one selling point they usually have in common is to tell us how much weight people lost in their first week. "I lost 6 pounds in just one week on this diet plan," or "In just one week, I lost 12 pounds", or "Lose 5 pounds by the end of your first week or your money back." These claims focus on the change that takes place in seven days. If this can happen with the physical body depending on what foods you eat, think about what can happen in just 7 days to your thinking when you make a choice to stop feeding your mind junk.

Here is what a 7-day 1,200 calorie meal plan might look like in comparison to a 7-day thought shifting exercise plan. The food plans are not presented for you to follow as you're doing the 7-day thought shifting but rather so you can compare and visualise right in front of you how the plans are similarly laid out. Pay close attention not only to what is suggested to eat, but the fact that portion size is of the utmost importance. This will apply to your thought-changing diet as well. Don't overwhelm yourself by jumping in and indulging in too much too soon. Likewise, don't starve your mind by trying to stifle negative thinking without replacing it with healthier food for thought.

Also keep in mind that any diet plan intended for weight loss is usually going to allow you to eat as much fresh vegetables as you want if you find that you are too hungry in between meals. This is because the veggies are low in calories but packed with nutrients, so you never fall off of the diet while you get more value than you would if you instead opted to grab a bag of crisps. The same is true with a thought-changing diet plan. Throughout the day, you may find that there are moments when you find yourself drifting into negative thought patterns or old habits that have proven to get you nowhere but down. Fill these moments instead with thought-shifting ideas to move your thinking to more positive thoughts, feeding your mind with more satisfying thinking.

Chapter Seven

A RECIPE FOR SUCCESS

Here are the sample plans side by side with a typical diet plan for weight loss right next to the 7-day thought lifting, life changing plan. Again, **please note** that the food diet plans are not listed here as any kind of recommendation for you to change your eating. They are only listed so you can compare how the two 7-day diets compare:

Food diet plan:

Day 1: Breakfast – Combine ¾ cup of bran flakes with one banana and a cup of skim milk.

Day 1: Lunch – Build a sandwich with one mini whole wheat pita pocket bread, 3 ounces of turkey breast, half roasted pepper, one teaspoon of mayo, mustard, and lettuce. Serve with one stick of skim mozzarella string cheese and 2 kiwis.

Day 1: Dinner – Serve 4 ounces broiled flounder or sole with two sliced plum tomatoes sprinkled with 2 tablespoons of grated Parmesan cheese, broiled until golden. Eat with one cup of cooked couscous and one cup of steamed broccoli. Enjoy it with a single serving of ice cream for dessert.

Thought diet plan:

Day 1: Morning – Wake up and think about how grateful you are that the sun came up and it is the start of a brand new day. Pour yourself a hot cup of coffee and think about how happy the smell makes you feel. Think about your plans for the day and focus on the achievements that will take place and the people you will encounter who will make you smile.

Day 1: Afternoon – Take a moment to walk to a quiet place to regroup your thoughts and to relax. Think about what you have accomplished in the half of a day you have been awake. Focus on the people around you who have made you feel as if it mattered that you showed up today.

Day 1: Evening – Right before you turn out the light to head for bed, take out your gratitude journal and begin jotting down a few thoughts that enriched your day. Look back over the entire day and write down the best part. Really focus on the people that made you feel like you belonged and are a success.

Food diet plan:

Day 2: Breakfast – Blend one cup of frozen berries with a half of a banana and 8 ounces of skim milk into a smoothie. Add one or two hard-boiled eggs for protein.

Day 2: Lunch – Eat one cup of vegetarian vegetable soup with one veggie burger on whole-grain toast with one cup of grapes

Day 2: Dinner – Rub 4 ounces of boneless skinless chicken breast with BBQ sauce and grill. Add two heaping cups of sauteed spinach with garlic, olive oil, and tomatoes and serve with half of a plain or sweet potato baked.

Thought diet plan:

Day 2: Morning – Before you get out of bed list 3 things you are looking forward to for the day inside your head. Think about someone you will encounter during the day who makes you feel important.

Day 2: Afternoon – Whenever a negative thought comes to mind, immediately look it up on the negative thoughts list and replace the thought with a positive one that is listed. Speak the positive thoughts out loud saying them at least three times each allowing yourself to hear them clearly.

Day 2: Evening – Look through pictures from happy times, and set some aside to focus on. Think about these memories as you drift off to sleep.

Food diet plan:

Day 3: Breakfast – Cook half a cup of quick oats with skim milk. Add half an apple, sliced or chopped with 1 teaspoon honey and a pinch of cinnamon.

Day 3: Lunch -Make chicken salad by tossing 4 ounces of shredded skinless roast chicken breast with ¼ cup of sliced red grapes, one tablespoon slivered almonds, one tablespoon mayo, and one tablespoon plain unsweetened Greek yogurt. Serve it on top of lettuce and a banana on the side.

Day 3: Dinner – steamed shrimp with one baked potato topped with 3 tablespoons of salsa and one tablespoon unsweetened Greek yogurt plus 3 cups spinach, steamed. Finish the meal off with a one ounce of chocolate or a low-calorie ice cream bar.

Thought diet plan:

Day 3: Morning – As you prepare for the day ahead, begin to speak out loud some affirmations that you would like to see come into fruition as your day unfolds.

Day 3: Afternoon – Throughout the day, be sure to capture every less-than-perfect thought as if you are trapping wild game or like a cat fixated on a mouse to pounce upon it. Use the negative/positive thinking list to help bring your thoughts into line quickly.

Day 3: Evening – Fill up the bath with warm water and maybe some bubbles and candles nearby. Relax in there before getting in pajamas to go to bed. Before you relax to sleep for the night, grab your gratitude journal and list out 3 things that made you laugh today.

Food diet plan:

Day 4: Breakfast – Top half an English muffin with half a small apple, sliced and one ounce shredded reduced-fat cheese. Microwave it for 30 seconds. Serve with 2/3 cup plain, unsweetened Greek yogurt sprinkled with slivered almonds.

Day 4: Lunch – Heat up a cup of tomato soup, and serve it with a sandwich made with one mini pita, 3 ounces thinly sliced roast beef, one teaspoon horseradish, mustard, tomato slices, and lettuce. Eat with 2 cups of raw veggies and ¼ cup of hummus.

Day 4: Dinner – Serve 4 ounces of poached salmon with slaw made by tossing 1 ¼ cups coleslaw mix with 2 sliced scallions with one tablespoon of rice vinegar and 1 ½ teaspoons olive oil. Add spices, herbs, and seasoning as desired. Pair with ¾ cup of 100% whole grain such as quinoa and an apple.

Thought diet plan:

Day 4: Morning – Start your day with a smile. After you have brushed your teeth, look into the mirror with the biggest smile you can manage.

Day 4: Afternoon - With every negative thought you notice today, as you transfer these thoughts to the optimistic side, try to use as many senses as you can to associate it with the new positive thinking. For instance, bite into a sweet grape as you speak the positive notion. If you are fortunate enough to live near a beach, walk letting the sand sift between your toes as you speak uplifting words with every step. Taste – Smell – Sight – Sound – Touch. Use as much of these senses as you can to make an association with each positive word.

Day 4: Evening – Before your head hits the pillow, take some time to put some happy thoughts into a song. It doesn't matter who is around to hear you, but if you are wanting a bit of privacy, sing in the shower. Regardless of where you choose to do so, just sing. Make sure the lyrics are uplifting and not something that will bring you down. Sing a song you know or simply put some good thoughts to a tune.

Food diet plan:

Day 5: Breakfast – Combine 1 cup of oats cereal with ½ cup berries and 1 tablespoon slivered almonds and 6 ounces plain unsweetened Greek yogurt.

Day 5: Lunch – Make a quesadilla by spreading ¼ cup of fat-free refried beans over a stone ground corn tortilla. Sprinkle on one ounce shredded skim cheese. Top with salsa and another tortilla. Microwave until cheese is melted and serve with cucumber spears and half cup of cottage cheese or Greek yogurt topped with 2 clementines.

Day 5: Dinner – 3 ounces roasted pork tenderloin with one cup baked acorn squash, mashed with a pinch of cinnamon, 2 to 3 cups of salad greens with a dash of olive oil and as much vinegar as you want to taste. Add chocolate or an ice cream bar for dessert.

Thought diet plan:

Day 5: Morning – As you put your feet on the ground for the first time, shifting from your cozy bed in the morning, think about the cause and effect and how it applies to your thoughts and circumstances as well. Just as you caused your feet to pivot out of a sleeping position to standing, you are causing your thoughts to pivot to result in changing your relationships, your health, and your finances.

Day 5: Afternoon - Notice throughout the day what time of day you tend to struggle the most with pressing into good thoughts. Figure out what causes this to be difficult, and adjust your behavior. For instance, do you start to feel pessimistic and grumpy in the mid afternoon when you are also starting to tire or have that mid afternoon sugar crash? Pay close attention to give yourself extra leeway during this part of your day. If you need a healthy snack to boost your sugar levels, then prepare for this. If you find that you begin to tire around a certain time of day, catch it early and take a break before the sleepies and weariness sets in.

Day 5: Evening – Get out your gratitude journal, and list out 3 things in your life that have been a result of cause and effect. Write down how thankful you are about the outcome and what caused this outcome to happen.

Food diet plan:

Day 6: Breakfast – Toast one whole-grain frozen waffle and spread it with 2 tablespoons of nut butter. Top with one small sliced banana plus cinnamon and nutmeg. Serve with 8 ounces of skim milk.

Day 6: Lunch – Make a tuna pita with one mini whole wheat pita, 2 ounces of water packed light tuna, one tablespoon mayo, mustard, cucumber, and onion slices. Serve with 10 baby carrots and 2/3 cup plain, unsweetened Greek yogurt with a small pear.

Day 6: Dinner – Make jambalaya by mixing ¾ cup cooked brown rice with ½ cup corn, 2 ounces cooked turkey sausage, sliced, 1/3 cup salsa and ¼ cup no-salt black or navy beans. Heat and eat with 3 cups spinach sauteed with garlic and one tablespoon olive oil.

Thought diet plan:

Day 6: Morning – Before you get out of bed, think about 5 things that you like about yourself. Give yourself permission to feel good today. Think about these characteristics that you like about yourself all day long. Every hour, stop and remind yourself of these good traits.

Day 6: Afternoon – Whenever a negative thought tries to take hold of your thinking, stop. Physically stop what you are doing, and begin to think about the truth of the positive aspects of these thoughts. Imagine how you hope to see this positively played out in your life.

Day 6: Evening – Close your eyes thinking about and reminding yourself of the 5 traits you chose this morning that you find to be positive about yourself.

Food diet plan:

Day 7: Breakfast – Layer half toasted English muffin with one ounce reduced-fat cheese, sliced, one tomato slice, one cup steamed spinach, drained, and one poached egg. Serve with one grapefruit.

Day 7: Lunch – Make black bean salad by tossing ½ cup canned black beans, ½ cup orange slices, chopped red bell peppers, red onion, scallions, and any other desired veggies with one teaspoon vinegar. Serve over salad greens. Serve with one 100% stone ground corn tortilla and a piece of fruit.

Day 7: Dinner – Serve 3 ounces broiled or grilled flank steak with one baked sweet potato and one teaspoon butter, one cup steamed zucchini and one and a half cup of berries.

Thought diet plan:

Day 7: Morning – As you open your eyes, think about how beautiful the sunrise is, how aromatic the coffee smells as the scent whiffs into your nose. Compliment yourself for your achievement of making it the full week improving your thoughts. Begin to look at areas of your life where things have begun to change as a result of more positive thoughts.

Day 7: Afternoon – As thoughts come to mind throughout the day, reflect upon how much easier it has become in just seven days to recognise negative thinking and switch it over the positive thinking.

Day 7: Evening – Before you head to bed, bring out your gratitude journal and review the things you have written inside during these 7 days.

What to expect

At the end of the week, what will look different? What will be different? You have begun the process of training your thinking to new levels. You have fed your mind the healthy thoughts it was craving. Now, the way you view the world will begin to look brighter, more hopeful. Instead of feeling discouraged and powerless, you will begin to realise you are living in a new reality. The picture of your life will have developed into something closer to what your heart desires.

Think of the entire process as that of a skilled photographer developing a picture.

In days before digital art and images, if you wanted your picture captured, you would have to do so on film. This film was then taken into a dark room and developed before it could be transferred to a special kind of photographic paper where it was printed into a picture you could frame or tuck away in a memory photo album to view as you pleased whenever you wanted.

Of course, first you needed a camera and film along with a nice backdrop and the perfect lighting. Too little light, or the wrong angle would put you sitting in darkness or cast a shadow on your face. Too much light would wash out the entire picture so nothing would be crisp or in focus. The photographer would set the shutter speed and aperture openings to further determine how much light would be allowed into the camera to be caught by the film inside.

To develop the film, you must first open up the camera in a room that is completely void of any light, a dark room. You will need a developing tank, reels, graduates, storage containers, film clips, a thermometer, stop watch or timer, chemical developer, fixer, and water. You would then load the film onto the reels, prepare the solution, place the reel into the developing tank, and then seal it shut allowing no light to enter. The photographic process transforms the latent image into a visible image onto a negative. The image will be inverted, showing up as dark spots that are really white, or colours that are opposite each other.

In the end, you take a negative and turn it into a positive image. Now, let's apply this to our seven-day thought changing process. You have pushed your mind beyond positive imaginations and have started the process of establishing a new reality.

You must form new habits of thought that are gained by laying a foundation in a matter of a few days. Purposely devote one week toward developing this new habit of thinking by transforming the negative to a positive again, or focusing on the opposite colour so you can see the full picture. Set it as a priority making everything else in that week less important. If you do this, it will be your turning point toward.

This new way of thinking doesn't mean you will no longer face trying times. What it will mean is that you will face these same circumstances with a new state of mind that will send the struggles running.

At the end of the week

Most discover that this week of training their thoughts leaves them with a new insightful way of looking at the world around them. This new way of thinking is so appealing that you will never want to turn back to your old, discouraging ways. Things will be different in a much improved and better way for the rest of your life.

Chapter Eight
PERSISTENCE IS THE KEY

What happens if I fail?

First of all, falling back into a pattern of dwelling on unpleasant thoughts will not make you fail. In fact, expect this to happen at least once throughout your week. If you become exhausted or struggle, drop the process all together for several days. Then, attempt it again. Just make sure you do not jump off and onto it too quickly. When it does happen, simply start again where you left off. However, allow yourself at least a few days in between stopping and starting after a lapse.

Negativity will bombard you

Chances are that as soon as you begin this 7-day thought-changing process, negativity will begin to bombard you. You will see a sad or discouraging news story. Your friends or co-workers will begin trying to get you to join in some awful gossip. You will probably see less than happy posts on social media. Your children or your spouse may even suddenly have all sorts of earth-shattering problems they want to discuss with you. The idea here is not that you lock yourself off from the world in the basement or in a cabin in the woods for a week, but rather that you do not entertain any of these negative thoughts. Let the negativity float around you in the atmosphere, but do not let it set into your mind or take hold of these thoughts to dwell on them. That's the secret to sustaining this 7-day thought-changing experience that will change your life.

Entertaining thoughts

What does it mean to entertain a negative thought or to take hold of it or dwell on it? Negativity is bound to happen all around us, but as soon as you are aware of these negative influences, refuse to take hold of them. Turn them out like an unwanted guest. Treat these unwanted thoughts like you would treat an unwanted visitor who comes knocking on your door. Ignore it, or turn it away. Do not allow it to come inside your mind. Don't give it a second thought. If the thought is negative, release it. Don't dwell upon it.

Be clear that potential thoughts are constantly going to be coming at us, bombarding us. It's up to us to decide which ones we will invite inside to entertain. Imagine you are at home and hear a knock on the door. Some people excitedly throw the door open to every knock or doorbell ring. Others might first view through a peep hole or observe the visitor on a video surveillance before making the choice to open up the door to them or leave them outside on the doorstep. While some visitors are going to be friendly, familiar faces that brighten our day, others will be strangers or even a threat to our safety. It is the potential thief or threatening visitor that we should not open up the door to. We should leave them outside safely on the other side of the locked door where they will be unable to do us any harm.

During this 7-day project, this is how we should treat negativity that tries to take hold of our thoughts. Treat them as a terrible threat to your peace. They will still try to enter your thinking, and they will succeed only if you allow them to do so. Once you let these negative thoughts inside, they will take hold and remind you of all of your failings. Do not let them do this. This is why the 7 days will be all it takes. It requires a great deal of energy to keep these thoughts at bay while you focus instead on enriching ones.

Releasing thoughts

While there are negative attacks on our thought processes that we must keep outside at any cost, there are also going to be thoughts that have already become trapped inside our thinking and need to be released. These thoughts, we need to clean out of our heads and set them free as we would a butterfly that has gone through the ugly chrysalis stage. If we choose not to release these thoughts, it will be like trapping a bat inside.

Take swift action

Just like you would quickly rush to put out a spark before it erupts into flames on your stove top or at a fuel pump, do not let negativity fester in your mind. Likewise, the first drop of rain may not seem like trouble, but when it collects with other raindrops, it can develop into a torrential downpour causing dangerous flooding. Turn it away from your thinking while it is still just a spark or drop of water. Otherwise, it will erupt and overflow into every area of your life, like a virus. The faster you turn away negativity that is trying to take root in your thinking, the better. Become aware of it only to the point of being able to turn your back on it. But, this doesn't mean you are rude to a friend. It does mean that if a news story is bothering you, turn off the news or put down the newspaper. If you see a complaining social media post, keep scrolling. Don't even consider commenting on it.

Do not be afraid

At this point, it's important to point out the fine line between recognising and taking a thought captive to toss it out before it festers and being fearful of them. Never fear these negative thoughts. To fear them means that you believe them, and this allows the negativity to have power in your thought life. Fear and anger often go hand in hand, so while you are combating these less than happy thoughts, be sure that you do not become indignant about them either.

Don't be moved

Some thoughts are going to drift into your racing mind, like catching a fluffy seed from a dandelion that a child has blown. Other thoughts are going to be handed to you during conversations or implied through the way someone is acting. Maybe you will receive a negative letter or phone call or text or see a sad headline. None of this matters so long as you don't entertain the negativity of it all. Immediately throw them out of your mind and begin to think about something else. Think of something pleasant. Do not give power to these negative influences or attempts to bring you down. Do not let these thoughts take hold of you.

When we entertain a thought or allow it to dwell in us, what we are doing is allowing the thought to move us. It is very important during these seven days that you do not allow your cares to move you or to affect you. This doesn't mean you become uncaring, fearfully, angrily or even awkwardly snub a negative friend. Simply, don't mentally accept what they are saying. However, if there is someone who tends to spur on less than positive thoughts in you, it will be helpful to avoid meeting with them during your seven-day project. If this is not possible, then wait until you can be apart from this person before you begin the week-long experience.

Never give your mental consent to negativity

It is not possible to entertain a thought without giving it our mental stamp of approval or consent. What we choose to think about is what we are feeding our minds. It becomes a diet for our minds. Refuse to give your mental consent. Refuse to accept negative news at face value. Instead, look for the good in the situation or assume the best until you know otherwise, and then turn the bad thoughts away.

You are not responsible for the world around you.

The moment you begin your week long thought-changing process, it will probably look as though everything around you is going wrong all of a sudden and all at once. Let it!

When the difficulties seem to be stirred up around us, this is actually a really good sign. When the world around you begins to shake and rock its foundation, this means you have touched upon something real. This is the time to just hold on tight. When the storm has passed, and the rocking is over, things will look clearer and closer to what your heart desires.

Don't allow yourself to focus on the chaos around you. Sometimes things have to rock before they shift into place. You are only responsible for the way you think and not for all of the things that are seeming to suddenly go wrong. Even if the whole world begins to shake and rock out of control, don't let it throw you off course. The truth is that nothing anyone else says can throw you off course. The only thing that will throw you off of the 7-day thinking process is your own reaction.

At the end of the week

You did it! The days came one day at a time until you reached the seventh day of the exercise. How are you feeling now? Has your mindset improved? Do you feel more balanced? Chances are these will be seven days that you will never forget. You will most likely be forever grateful for the opportunity to set aside this week, just seven days of intense focus, to retrain your thinking. In return, expect more than your thinking to have changed. You will start to notice that the circumstances in your life have started changing for the better as well.

This 7-day process is so mentally challenging that you will not be able to go through it longer than a week. But, don't worry! A week is plenty of time to change your mind for the better. By the end of the week of focused shift in thinking, you will notice some changes that have come into your life. These changes will reshape your future for success.

Refresher

Occasionally, set the 7-day project into motion again as a refresher from time to time. Whenever you notice your thoughts beginning to drift back into unproductive thinking, start the week-long process again. Take the power back and put it into a state of balance.

Embrace your new reality

Do not deny reality. However, don't assume that how things appear to be is reality. Refuse to take the negative appearance as the reality. Instead, as your thought processes begin to change away from negatively viewing the world, begin to embrace your new reality.

Other services:

Motivational Training & Speaking

Leadership Training

Change Management

Results based Strategies

Breakthrough Therapy

Client & Staff Engagement Program

Troubleshooting

If you have any issues that we may assist you with, please email info@theprivatementor.com and we can discuss,design and plan a specific program that suits your personal or business requirements.

Printed in Great Britain
by Amazon

43368097R00078